COMPUTER

SELF HELP TRAINING GUIDE

vol.2

A comprehensive and simplified step by step guide to computer appreciation with practical approach For Colleges and secondary schools

Benjamin Alex

Table of content

GENERAL CONCLUSION ON MICROSOFT OFFICE PACKAGES

Introduction to Microsoft Office

Microsoft Office is a suite of productivity applications developed by Microsoft. It includes several software programs that are commonly used in both personal and professional settings as seen below;

Microsoft Word: This word processing program is used for creating and formatting documents, such as letters, reports, and resumes.

Microsoft Excel: Excel is a spreadsheet program used for organizing and analyzing data..

Microsoft PowerPoint: PowerPoint is a presentation program used to create slideshows for meetings, conferences, and educational purposes.

Microsoft Outlook: Outlook is an email client and personal information manager that allows users to send and receive emails, manage calendars, contacts, and tasks.
Microsoft Access: Access is a database management system used for building and managing databases.

Microsoft OneNote: OneNote is a digital note-taking program that allows users to capture and organize notes, ideas, and information.

Microsoft Publisher: Publisher is a desktop publishing program used for creating professional-looking publications like brochures, flyers, and newsletters.

Microsoft SharePoint: SharePoint is a web-based collaboration platform that allows users to share and manage documents, collaborate on projects, and build websites.

Introduction to Microsoft word

Microsoft Word is a widely used word processing program developed by Microsoft Corporation. It is a part of the Microsoft Office suite, which includes other popular productivity software like Excel, PowerPoint, and Outlook.

Introduced in 1983, Microsoft Word quickly gained popularity and has since become one of the most widely used word processors worldwide. It is known for its user-friendly interface, powerful editing tools, and extensive formatting options. Whether you are a student, professional, writer, or anyone who needs to create or edit documents, Microsoft Word offers a robust set of features to help you accomplish your tasks efficiently.

With Microsoft Word, users can create, format, and edit text documents with ease. It provides a wide range of formatting options for text, paragraphs, and even entire documents, allowing users to customize their documents based on their specific needs. From changing font styles and sizes to using different alignment options, Microsoft Word offers a plethora of tools for creating visually appealing and well-structured documents.

Aside from basic formatting options, users can also insert various elements into their documents, such as images, shapes, tables, and hyperlinks. This allows for more dynamic and interactive content creation. Whether you need to include charts and graphs in a report or insert images and diagrams in a presentation, Microsoft Word provides the flexibility and functionality to enhance your documents.

Collaboration is made easy with Microsoft Word, as it allows multiple users to work on the same document simultaneously. This feature is particularly useful in professional settings, where documents often require input and feedback from multiple team members. Microsoft Word also provides features like comments and track changes, enabling effective communication and collaboration during the editing and review process.

Furthermore, Microsoft Word offers tools for proofreading and language checking to ensure that your documents are error-free. With its built-in spell checker and grammar checker, you can easily identify and correct any mistakes or inconsistencies in your text. Additionally, Word provides an extensive dictionary and thesaurus, making it a comprehensive writing tool.

With its extensive features, user-friendly interface, and compatibility with other Microsoft Office applications, Microsoft Word has become the go-to word processor for individuals and organizations worldwide. Whether you need to create professional documents, write a letter, draft a report, or simply take notes, Microsoft Word provides a reliable and efficient platform to handle all your word processing needs.

How to open Microsoft word program on your windows system

To open Microsoft Word on your Windows system, you can follow these steps:

1. Click on the "Start" button located at the bottom left corner of the screen. This will open the Start Menu.

2. Scroll through the list of installed applications until you find the "Microsoft Office" folder.

3. Click on the folder to expand it, and then click on the "Microsoft Word" icon.

4. Alternatively, you can also search for "Microsoft Word" in the search bar located at the bottom of the Start Menu. Simply type "Microsoft Word" and select the program from the search results.

5. Another method is to use the desktop shortcut if you have one. Look for the Microsoft Word icon on your desktop and double-click on it to open the program.

6. Once you click on the Microsoft Word icon or shortcut, the program will open, and you can start creating or editing your documents.

Overview of the Microsoft Word User Interface

The Microsoft Word user interface is designed to be user-friendly and intuitive, providing easy access to a wide range of features and tools. Here are some components of the Microsoft Word user interface:

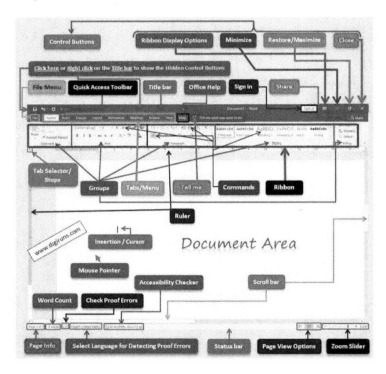

1. **Ribbon**: The Ribbon is the main toolbar located at the top of the screen. It consists of several tabs, such as Home, Insert, Page Layout, References, Review, and View. Each tab contains different groups of commands related to specific tasks or functions.

2. **Quick Access Toolbar**: The Quick Access Toolbar is a customizable toolbar located above the Ribbon. It allows you to add frequently used commands for quick access, such as Save, Undo, Redo, and Print.

3. **File tab**: The File tab is located at the top left corner of the screen. Clicking on it opens the Backstage View, where you can access functions like creating a new document, opening existing documents, saving, printing, and more.

4. **Document area**: The document area is the main workspace where you can view and edit your documents. It occupies the majority of the screen and displays your text and formatting.

5. **Status bar**: The status bar is located at the bottom of the screen. It provides information such as the current page number, word count, language settings, and zoom level. It also includes buttons for various view options, like Print Layout, Full Screen, and Web Layout.

6. **Formatting options**: Microsoft Word provides a range of formatting options in the Ribbon. You can change fonts, font sizes, apply bold, italics, underline, and change paragraph alignment, line spacing, and indentation.

7. **Navigation pane**: The Navigation pane is an optional panel on the left side of the screen. It allows you to navigate through your document using headings, pages, or search keywords.

8. **Insertion point**: The insertion point is a blinking vertical bar that indicates where your text will be inserted. It moves as you type or move around in your document using the keyboard or mouse.

Creating a new document in Microsoft word

To create a new document in Microsoft Word, follow these steps:

- **Launch Microsoft Word**.
  In the Word interface, you will typically see a blank document ready for you to start typing. If not, click on the File tab and select "New" to open a blank document.

- If you prefer to use a pre-designed document layout, you can choose a template. Click on the File tab and select "New." In the New Document pane, browse through the available templates or use the search bar to find a specific template. Double-click on the template to open a new document based on it.

- After creating the new document, save your work by clicking on the File tab and selecting "Save" or pressing Ctrl+S. Choose a location on your computer, give the document a name, and click "Save."

- Adjust any necessary document settings by going to the File tab, selecting "Options," and navigating relevant tabs. Customize default settings, such as font or spelling and grammar check options, as desired.

- Begin adding content to the document by clicking on the blank page and typing. Use the formatting options available in the Ribbon at the top of the screen to adjust font styles, paragraph alignment, and more.

- Customize the document further by adjusting page layout settings, inserting headers and footers, adding images and tables, applying styles and themes, and more. Explore the options available in the Ribbon to enhance your document.

- Remember to save your progress periodically by clicking on the Save button or using the Ctrl+S shortcut. It is also a good idea to save multiple versions or make regular backups of your document.

By following these steps, you can easily create a new document in Microsoft Word and begin working on your content.

Saving a document in Microsoft word

To save a document in Microsoft Word, follow these steps:

- After creating or making changes to a document, click on the File tab located in the top-left corner of the Word interface.

- The Backstage View will open, displaying various options. Select "Save" from the list.

- If you have already saved the document before, Word will automatically save it with the same file name and location. If you are working on a new document that hasn't been saved yet, or if you want to save it with a different name or in a different location, you will see the "Save As" dialog box.

- In the "Save As" dialog box, choose the location on your computer where you want to save the document. You can select a default location, such as the Documents folder, or choose a different folder by navigating through the folders on your computer.

- Type a name for the document in the "File name" field. Choose a descriptive and recognizable name that will make it easy to identify the document later.

- Select the desired file format from the "Save as type" dropdown menu. The default format is usually "Word Document (.docx)," which is the most commonly used format. However, you can also choose other formats such as "Word 97-2003 Document (.doc)" or "PDF (.pdf)" if needed.

- If desired, you can add tags or properties to the document by clicking on the "More options" arrow in the lower-left corner of the "Save As" dialog box. This allows you to specify details about the document, such as author name, keywords, or other metadata.

- Once you have chosen the location, name, and format, click on the "Save" button to save the document. Word will update the saved document and keep it stored in the selected location.

- It is recommended to save your document frequently while working on it to avoid losing any progress.

- You can use the Ctrl+S keyboard shortcut to quickly save the document at any time.

- Additionally, after the initial save, you can click the Save button on the Quick Access Toolbar, located at the top of the Word window, for quick and easy saving

Formatting Text in Microsoft Word

To format text in Microsoft Word, follow these steps:

- Select the text you want to format by clicking and dragging your cursor over the desired text. Alternatively, you can place the cursor at a specific location and then use the arrow keys to select the desired amount of text.

- Once the text is selected, use the formatting options on the Home tab in the Ribbon, located at the top of the Word window. The most commonly used formatting options are:

  1. Font: Click on the Font dropdown menu to choose a specific font for the selected text. You can also change the font size by selecting a size from the Font Size dropdown menu or manually entering a value.

  2. Bold, Italic, and Underline: Use the B, I, and U buttons respectively to apply or remove these formatting styles from the selected text. You can also click the small arrow next to each button to access additional formatting options.

  3. Alignment: Use the alignment buttons to align the text to the left, center, right, or justified (aligned to both the left and right margins) within the document.

  4. Bullets and Numbering: Use these buttons to create bulleted or numbered lists. Select the desired text and then click on the bulleted or numbered list button to apply the formatting. You can also click the small arrow next to each button to access additional formatting options.

  5. Text color and Highlight color: Use the Text Color and Highlight Color buttons to change the color of the selected text or apply a background color.

- You can also access additional formatting options by clicking on the small arrow in the lower-right corner of the Font or Paragraph section on the Home tab. This will open the Font or Paragraph dialog boxes, where you can further customize the formatting of the selected text.

- Additionally, you can use keyboard shortcuts to quickly apply formatting. For example, to apply bold formatting, select the text and press Ctrl+B. Similarly, press Ctrl+I to apply italics and Ctrl+U to underline.

- Remember to continuously save your document as you make formatting changes to ensure that your work is preserved.

Editing Text in Microsoft word

To edit text in Microsoft Word, follow these steps:

1. Open the Microsoft Word document you want to edit.

2. Select the text you want to edit by clicking and dragging your cursor over the desired text.

3. Once the text is selected, you can make changes in the following ways:

- To delete the selected text, press the Backspace or Delete key on your keyboard.

- To add new text, simply start typing after the selected text. The new text will be inserted at the cursor position.

- To format the text, use the toolbar at the top of the screen. You can change the font, font size, alignment, and apply various formatting styles.

- To cut, copy, or paste the selected text, right-click on the selected text and choose the appropriate option from the context menu, or use the keyboard shortcuts (Ctrl+X for cut, Ctrl+C for copy, and Ctrl+V for paste).

- To undo or redo any changes, click on the Undo or Redo button in the toolbar or use the keyboard shortcuts (Ctrl+Z for undo and Ctrl+Y for redo).

- To find and replace specific text, click on the "Find" button in the toolbar or use the Ctrl+F keyboard shortcut. You can then enter the text you want to find and the text you want to replace it with.

4. After making the desired changes, save your document by clicking on the File menu and selecting "Save" or using the Ctrl+S keyboard shortcut.

5. Remember to regularly save your document to avoid losing any changes.

Formatting paragraphs in Microsoft Word

Here are the steps on how to format paragraphs in Microsoft Word:

1. Select the paragraphs that you want to format. You can select one or more paragraphs by clicking and dragging your mouse over the text, or by using keyboard shortcuts such as Ctrl+A to select all the text in the document.

2. On the Home tab, in the Paragraph group, you can use the following buttons to adjust the basic formatting of your paragraphs:

- Align Left: Aligns the text to the left margin of the page.

- Center: Aligns the text to the center of the page.

- Align Right: Aligns the text to the right margin of the page.

- Justify: Aligns the text to both the left and right margins of the page, adding extra space between words as needed.

- Line and Paragraph Spacing: Allows you to change the amount of space between lines and paragraphs. You can choose from predefined options or customize your own settings

- Shading: Allows you to fill the background of your paragraphs with a color or a pattern.

- Borders: Allows you to add a border around your paragraphs. You can choose from different styles, colors, and widths of the border.

3. To access more options for paragraph formatting, click on the small arrow in the bottom right corner of the Paragraph group. This will open the Paragraph dialog box, where you can adjust the following settings:

- Indentation: Allows you to change the distance between your paragraphs and the margins of the page. You can use the Left and Right boxes to set a fixed indentation, or use the Special drop-down menu to choose from different types of indentation, such as First line or Hanging/

- Spacing: Allows you to change the amount of space before and after your paragraphs. You can use this to create more separation between different sections of your document.

- Line and Page Breaks: Allows you to control how your paragraphs break across pages. You can use this to prevent single lines or words from being separated from the rest of your paragraph, or to keep related paragraphs together on the same page.

- Click OK to apply your changes and close the dialog box.

4. You can also use paragraph styles to apply consistent formatting to your document. Paragraph styles are predefined sets of formatting options that you can apply to your paragraphs with one click. To use paragraph styles, follow these steps:

- On the Home tab, in the Styles group, you can see a gallery of different styles that are available for your document. You can hover over each style to see a preview of how it will look on your text, or click on the More button to see all the styles in a list.

- To apply a style to your selected paragraphs, simply click on the style that you want. You can also use keyboard shortcuts such as Ctrl+Shift+S to open the Apply Styles dialog box, where you can type in the name of the style that you want and press Enter.

- To modify an existing style or create a new one, right-click on the style that you want to change or base your new style on, and select Modify or New Style from the menu. This will open the Modify Style or Create New Style dialog box, where you can adjust various formatting options for your style.

You can also give your style a name and choose whether it is based on another style or linked to another style.

- Click OK to save your changes and close the dialog box.

Inserting elements in Microsoft Word

To insert various elements in Microsoft Word, including images, tables, charts, shapes, headers, footers, page numbers, and more, follow these steps:

1. Open the Microsoft Word document where you want to insert an element.

2. To insert an image, click on the "Insert" tab in the toolbar and then click on the "Picture" button. Browse your computer for the image you want to insert and click "Insert." You can also use the "Online Pictures" option to search and insert images from online sources.

3. To insert a table, click on the "Insert" tab, and then click on the "Table" button. Choose the number of rows and columns for your table or draw a custom table using the "Insert Table" option.

4. To insert a chart, click on the "Insert" tab, and then click on the "Chart" button. Choose the type of chart you want to create and enter your data in the chart data sheet.

5. To insert a shape, click on the "Insert" tab, and then click on the "Shapes" button. Select the desired shape from the drop-down menu and click and drag on the document to draw the shape.

6. To insert a header or a footer, click on the "Insert" tab, and then click on the "Header" or "Footer" button. Choose from the pre-designed header and footer styles or click on "Edit Header" or "Edit Footer" to customize your own. You can add text, page numbers, dates, and other elements within the header or footer section.

7. To insert page numbers, click on the "Insert" tab, and then click on the "Page Number" button. Choose the desired position and format for the page numbers.

8. To insert additional elements like text boxes, symbols, equations, and more, click on the "Insert" tab and explore the various options within the toolbar.

9. After inserting an element, you can customize it by selecting it and using the formatting options available in the toolbar.

10.Remember to save your document regularly by clicking on the File menu and selecting "Save" or using the Ctrl + S keyboard shortcut.

Reviewing and proofreading Documents in Microsoft Word

To review and proofread documents in Microsoft Word, follow these steps:

1. Open the Microsoft Word document you want to review and proofread.

2. Click on the "Review" tab in the toolbar. This tab contains all the necessary tools for reviewing and proofreading.

3. Use the "Spelling & Grammar" button to check for spelling and grammar errors. Click on it, and Microsoft Word will highlight potential errors and suggest corrections. Review each suggestion and make necessary changes.

4. Utilize the "Thesaurus" button to find synonyms for words or to avoid word repetition. Select a word and click on the "Thesaurus" button to see a list of alternative words. Choose the most appropriate one.

5. To insert comments in the document, select the text you want to comment on, then click on the "New Comment" button. A comment box will appear in the margin where you can type your comment. This is useful for providing feedback, asking questions, or suggesting edits.

6. If you want to track changes made during the review process, enable the "Track Changes" feature by clicking on the "Track Changes" button. Any changes you make in the document will be highlighted and displayed as "Markup." This feature allows you to easily identify changes and accept or reject them.

7. Use the "Comments" button to manage and navigate through the comments you have inserted. You can view, respond to, or delete comments within this section.

8. To compare two versions of a document, click on the "Compare" button. Select the original document and the revised document, and Word will generate a comparison showing the differences between the two.

9. If you want to restrict access or editing permissions for the document, click on the "Protect Document" button. You can choose to restrict formatting, editing, or add a password to protect the file from unauthorized changes.

10. Once you have completed the reviewing and proofreading process, go through the document one final time to ensure everything looks and reads correctly.

11. Remember to save your document regularly by clicking on the File menu and selecting "Save" or using the Ctrl + S keyboard shortcut.

Printing Files in Microsoft Word

To print files in Microsoft Word, follow these steps:

1. Open the Microsoft Word document you want to print.

2. Click on the File tab in the top left corner of the screen.

3. In the File menu, select the "Print" option. Alternatively, you can use the Ctrl + P keyboard shortcut.

4. The Print dialog box will appear, showing a preview of how the document will look when printed.

5. Review the settings in the Print dialog box to ensure they are set according to your preferences. Here are some options you may want to check:

- Printer: Select the printer you want to use from the drop-down menu. If you have multiple printers installed, make sure you choose the correct one.

- Page Range: By default, Word will print the entire document. If you only want to print specific pages, select the appropriate page range option, such as "All," "Current Page," or "Pages." Enter the page numbers or ranges in the provided box.

- Copies: Specify the number of copies you want to print. Use the up and down arrows or type a number manually.

- Printer Properties: Click on the "Printer Properties" or "Preferences" button to access additional options specific to your printer, such as paper size, orientation, paper source, print quality, etc.

6. Once you have reviewed and adjusted the settings, click on the "Print" button at the bottom of the Print dialog box to start the printing process.

7. Wait for your document to print. Depending on the size of the document and the printer's speed, this may take a few moments.

8. After printing, collect your printed document from the printer's output tray.

Note: If you encounter any printing issues, such as the document not printing correctly or the printer not working, ensure that your printer is properly connected and turned on. You may also want to check if you have the latest printer drivers installed.

By following these steps, you can easily print files in Microsoft Word to have physical copies of your documents.

The use of styles in Microsoft Word

The use of styles in Microsoft Word can greatly enhance the formatting and organization of your documents. Styles are sets of formatting options that can be applied to text, paragraphs, headings, and other elements in your document. They provide consistency, efficiency, and flexibility in managing the appearance of your content.

Here are some key benefits and uses of styles in Microsoft Word:

1. **Consistency**: By applying styles to your document, you can ensure consistent formatting throughout. Any changes made to a style will automatically update all instances of that style within the document. This saves you time and effort in manually adjusting formatting.

2. **Efficiency**: Styles allow you to quickly format your text and paragraphs without individually selecting and applying different formatting options. With a few clicks, you can apply a desired style to any text or paragraph, giving your document a professional and polished look.

3. **Organization**: Using styles, you can structure your document with headings and subheadings, creating a logical and hierarchical outline. This is particularly useful for generating a table of contents and navigating lengthy documents. You can easily apply different heading styles to your headings, and Word will automatically generate a table of contents based on these styles.

4. **Quick changes**: If you decide to change the formatting of specific elements in your document, such as font type, font size, spacing, or indents, you can simply modify the associated style, and the changes will be reflected throughout the document. This eliminates the need to manually update each instance.

5. **Customization**: Microsoft Word provides pre-designed styles, such as Heading styles, Title styles, and Body styles. However, you can also create your own custom styles to meet your specific formatting needs. This allows you to adapt Word's built-in styles or create entirely new styles that reflect your preferred formatting preferences.

To use styles in Microsoft Word, follow these steps:

1. Open Microsoft Word and open the document you want to format.

2. Select the text or paragraph that you want to format with a style. You can do this by clicking and dragging your cursor over the text, or by placing your cursor within the paragraph.

3. On the Home tab of the ribbon, locate the "Styles" group. This group contains various styles that you can apply to your text or paragraphs.

4. Click the small arrow or dropdown button in the bottom right corner of the Styles group to open the Styles pane.

5. In the Styles pane, you will see a list of different styles organized by categories such as "Normal," "Heading," "Title," and more. Hover your cursor over a style to see a preview of how it will look in your document.

6. Click on the style that you want to apply. The selected text or paragraph will now be formatted according to the chosen style.

7. To modify an existing style, right-click on the style in the Styles pane and select "Modify" from the context menu. This will open the "Modify Style" dialog box, where you can make changes to the font, size, color, spacing, alignment, and other formatting options. Click "OK" to save your changes.

8. To create a new custom style, click the "New Style" button in the Styles pane. This will open the "Create New Style from Formatting" dialog box. Give your new style a name, and then specify the desired formatting options. Click "OK" to create the new style.

9. To apply a style to a heading or create a table of contents based on your styled headings, use the built-in Heading styles. Apply the appropriate Heading style to each heading in your document, and then go to the location where you want to insert the table of contents. On the References tab, click "Table of Contents" and select the desired style.

10. Repeat the above steps to apply additional styles to your document, ensuring consistency and a professional appearance throughout your content.

Creating tables of contents in Microsoft Word

To create a table of contents in Microsoft Word, follow these steps:

1. Place your cursor in the location where you want to insert the table of contents.

2. On the ribbon, go to the "References" tab.

3. In the "Table of Contents" group, click on the "Table of Contents" button. This will open a dropdown menu with various options for creating a table of contents.

4. To create a basic table of contents, select one of the automatic styles listed in the dropdown menu. The available styles might include "Automatic Table 1" or "Automatic Table 2". These styles will automatically generate a table of contents based on the headings in your document, using the built-in Heading styles.

5. If you want to customize the appearance or formatting of the table of contents, select the "Custom Table of Contents" option from the dropdown menu.

6. In the "Table of Contents" dialog box that appears, you can make various customizations. For example, you can choose how many levels of headings to include in the table of contents, format the appearance of the table of contents, and modify the tab leader style.

7. Once you have made your desired customizations, click "OK". The table of contents will be inserted into your document.

8. If you make changes to the headings in your document, such as adding, removing, or reordering them, you can update the table of contents by right-clicking on the table of contents and selecting "Update Field" from the context menu. Choose the "Update entire table" option to update all the entries in the table of contents.

Using these steps, you can easily create a table of contents in Microsoft Word, either with automatic styles or customized settings to suit your specific document formatting needs.

Formatting with themes in Microsoft Word

To format your document with themes in Microsoft Word, follow these steps:

1. Open Microsoft Word and open the document you want to format.

2. On the ribbon, go to the "Design" tab. This tab contains various options for formatting your document with themes.

3. In the "Themes" group, you will see a selection of pre-designed themes. Hover your cursor over a theme to see a live preview of how it will look in your document.

4. Click on the theme that you want to apply. The selected theme will be applied to your entire document, including fonts, colors, and effects.

5. To further customize the theme, click on the "Colors" button in the "Themes" group. This will open a dropdown menu with different color schemes that are available within the selected theme. Choose the one that suits your preferences.

6. If you want to change the fonts used in the theme, click on the "Fonts" button in the "Themes" group. This will open a dropdown menu where you can choose from different font sets that are part of the selected theme. Select the font set you prefer.

7. To modify the effects applied by the theme, such as shadows or lines, click on the "Effects" button in the "Themes" group. This will open a dropdown menu with different effect styles that are part of the selected theme. Select the style you want to apply.

8. You can also adjust the theme elements individually by going to the "Page Background" group in the "Design" tab. Here, you can change the page color, apply a watermark, or choose a different page border.

9. If you want to save your customized theme for future use, click on the "More" button in the "Themes" group and select "Save Current Theme". Give your theme a name and click "Save".

10. To switch to a different theme or revert to the default theme, simply go back to the "Design" tab and choose a different theme from the available options.

By following these steps, you can easily format your document with themes in Microsoft Word, giving it a cohesive and professional look.

Conclusion on Microsoft Office Word

This training package for Microsoft Word will provide you with the valuable skills and knowledge that can greatly improve your productivity and efficiency when working with documents. From basic formatting and editing to advanced features such as themes and templates, this training equips you with the necessary tools to create professional-level documents.

By mastering the various tools and techniques taught in the training, you can save time and effort in formatting and organizing your documents. The training covers a wide range of topics, offering step-by-step instructions and hands-on practice to ensure a solid understanding of Microsoft Word.

With the skills acquired from this training, you will be better equipped to create visually appealing and polished documents, from simple letters and memos to complex reports and presentations.

Microsoft Word is one of the most widely used word processing tools, and by becoming proficient in it, you will feel confident in your ability to create professional documents in any professional or academic setting.

In conclusion, the general training package for Microsoft Word is a valuable investment in your professional development, empowering you to harness the full potential of this powerful software and ultimately enhancing your document creation and editing capabilities.

Introduction to Microsoft Excel

Microsoft Excel is a powerful spreadsheet program that allows users to perform complex calculations, analyze data, and create visually appealing charts and graphs. Whether you're a beginner or an experienced user, Excel provides a wide range of functionalities that can help streamline your work, improve efficiency, and make data-driven decisions.

Excel is part of the Microsoft Office suite, which includes other popular productivity tools such as Word, PowerPoint, and Outlook. It is widely used in various industries, including finance, accounting, marketing, human resources, and many others. Its versatility and flexibility make it an essential tool for professionals across different fields.

The Excel interface is user-friendly and consists of a grid of cells arranged in columns and rows. Each cell can contain text, numbers, formulas, or functions. These cells can be referenced in calculations or used to organize and store data. Excel provides a wide range of built-in functions that perform various mathematical, statistical, and logical operations, making it a powerful tool for data analysis.

One of Excel's key features is its ability to create dynamic formulas, allowing users to perform calculations on large sets of data with ease. These formulas can be as simple as adding two numbers together or as complex as analyzing and manipulating large datasets. Excel also allows users to format and customize their worksheets to make the data more visually appealing and easier to understand.

Excel also offers advanced features such as pivot tables, which allow users to summarize and analyze large datasets quickly. Pivot tables can generate interactive reports, enabling users to easily filter and analyze data from multiple perspectives. Excel's charting capabilities also make it easy to visually represent data through various chart types, including bar charts, line graphs, and pie charts.

Collaboration and sharing are made easy with Excel's ability to protect worksheets and workbooks, track changes, and share files with others. Users can also use macros to automate repetitive tasks or create custom functions to extend Excel's functionality.

In conclusion, Microsoft Excel is a versatile and powerful tool that can be used for a wide range of tasks, from simple calculations to complex data analysis. By learning how to effectively use the features and functionalities offered by Excel, individuals can become more efficient and productive in their work, making better-informed decisions based on data-driven insights.

Exploring the Excel interface

When you first open Microsoft Excel, you will be greeted with a clean and organized interface designed to help you navigate and manipulate your data effectively. Let's explore the main components of the Excel interface:

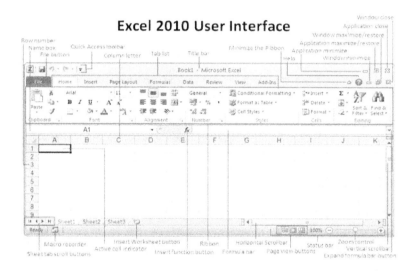

Ribbon: At the top of the Excel window, you will find the Ribbon, which is divided into tabs such as Home, Insert, Formulas, Data, Review, and View. These tabs contain various commands and tools to perform different tasks in Excel. Each tab is further divided into groups, making it easy to locate specific commands.

Quick Access Toolbar: Located above the Ribbon, the Quick Access Toolbar provides quick access to commonly used commands, such as Save, Undo, and Redo. You can customize this toolbar by adding or removing commands according to your preferences.

Workbook: In Excel, a workbook is a file that contains one or more worksheets. By default, a new workbook opens with three blank worksheets, which you can rename and organize as needed. You can also add additional worksheets or delete existing ones as required.

Worksheet: This is where you enter and manipulate your data. Each worksheet consists of a grid of cells organized into columns (identified by letters) and rows (identified by numbers). You can navigate through the worksheet using the arrow keys or by clicking on the desired cell.

Formula Bar: Located above the worksheet grid, the Formula Bar displays the contents of the selected cell, allowing you to enter and edit formulas, functions, or text. It also shows the results of calculations performed on the selected cell or range of cells.

Cell: A cell is the intersection of a column and a row in the worksheet grid. It can contain different types of data, such as text, numbers, formulas, or functions. Each cell has its unique address, referred to as a cell reference, which is identified by the column letter and row number.

Columns and Rows: Columns run vertically from the top of the worksheet, identified by letters from A to Z and continuing with double letters, such as AA, AB, etc. Rows run horizontally from the left side of the worksheet, identified by numbers. You can adjust the width and height of columns and rows to accommodate your data by dragging the separators between them.

Sheet Tabs: At the bottom of the Excel window, you will find sheet tabs that represent each worksheet in the workbook. You can switch between worksheets by clicking on the corresponding tab. You can also add new sheets, duplicate existing ones, or delete unwanted sheets.

Status Bar: Located at the bottom of the Excel window, the Status Bar provides information about the current status of Excel and displays useful tools like zoom, page layout, and calculations mode. You can customize the status bar by right-clicking on it and selecting the desired options.

Help and Assistance: If you need help while working in Excel, you can access various resources by clicking on the question mark icon in the top-right corner of the Excel window. Here you will find options for accessing the Excel Help feature, viewing online tutorials, and contacting customer support.

Navigating and understanding the Excel interface is essential to effectively use the software's features and functionalities. By familiarizing yourself with the main components and their functions, you will be able to navigate through your data, perform calculations, and create visually appealing reports and charts with ease.

Understanding the differences between a workbook and a worksheet

In Excel, a workbook and a worksheet are two different components of the program with distinct purposes:

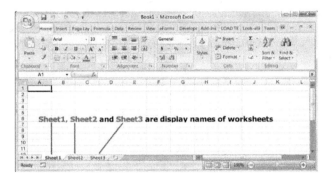

Workbook: A workbook is the main container that holds all of your data and worksheets. It is essentially an Excel file that can contain multiple worksheets. Each workbook is saved as a separate file on your computer. Workbooks can be created, opened, edited, and saved in Excel.

Worksheet: A worksheet is a single sheet within a workbook that is used to organize and manipulate data. It is a grid-like structure consisting of rows, columns, and cells. Worksheets are where you input and analyze your data, perform calculations, and create charts or graphs. By default, a new workbook starts with one worksheet, but you can add, delete, and rename worksheets to suit your needs.

Therefore, a workbook is the entire file that contains multiple worksheets, while a worksheet is an individual sheet within the workbook where you enter and work with data. Workbooks can have multiple worksheets, but each worksheet is a separate entity within the workbook.

Navigating worksheets and workbooks in Excel

When working with multiple worksheets or workbooks in Excel, it's important to know how to navigate between them efficiently. Excel provides several ways to move between worksheets and workbooks to access the data you need. Here are some methods for navigating worksheets and workbooks in Excel:

Switching between worksheets in the same workbook:

1. Use the sheet tabs at the bottom of the Excel window. Simply click on the tab of the desired worksheet to switch to it.

2. Use the keyboard shortcuts. Press Ctrl+PgUp to move to the previous worksheet and Ctrl+PgDn to move to the next worksheet.

Navigating quickly within a worksheet:

1. Use the arrow keys on your keyboard to move to adjacent cells.

2. Press Ctrl+Home to move to the upper-left corner of the worksheet.

3. Press Ctrl+End to move to the last cell of the worksheet that contains data.

Moving or copying worksheets within a workbook:

1. Right-click on the sheet tab you want to move or copy and select "Move or Copy" from the context menu. Then, choose the location where you want the sheet to be moved or copied to.

2. You can also move or copy worksheets by holding down the Ctrl key, clicking and dragging the sheet tab to the desired location within the workbook.

Switching between workbooks:

1. Click on the "View" tab in the Ribbon, and then click on "Switch Windows." This will show a list of all open workbooks, allowing you to select the one you want to switch to.

2. Use the keyboard shortcut Ctrl+Tab to cycle through the open workbooks.

Creating links between worksheets and workbooks:

1. You can create hyperlinks within your worksheets to jump to specific cells or locations in other worksheets or workbooks. To do this, highlight the cell where you want to create the hyperlink, right-click, and select "Hyperlink." Then, specify the location of the cell or file you want to link to.

2. You can also use formulas to reference cells or ranges in other worksheets or workbooks. Simply enter the equals sign (=) followed by the cell or range reference in the formula bar.

By mastering these navigation techniques, you will be able to navigate and work efficiently with multiple worksheets and workbooks in Excel. It will help you quickly access and analyze your data, improving your productivity and effectiveness in using Excel.

Understanding Cells in Excel

Cells are the basic building blocks of Microsoft Excel. They are the small rectangular boxes within the worksheet grid where you can enter different types of data, such as text, numbers, formulas, or functions. Each cell has a unique address, referred to as a cell reference, which is identified by the column letter and row number.

◢	A	B	C	D	E	F
1		3/31/2016	6/30/2016	9/30/2016	12/31/2016	
2	Income					
3	Lemonade	3000	3100	3200	3300	
4	Cookies	000	2200	2400	2600	
5	Total Income					
6	Expense					
7	Payroll		Cell B3 is selected			
8	Marketing					
9	Supplies					
10	Total Expense					
11	Net Income					
12						

Here are some key points to understand about cells in Excel:

1. **Cell Reference**: Each cell in Excel has a specific cell reference that helps you identify and locate it within the worksheet grid. The cell reference consists of a combination of the column letter and the row number. For example, the cell in the first column and first row is referred to as cell A1.

2. **Data Types**: Cells in Excel can hold various types of data. You can enter text, numbers, dates, or formulas to perform calculations. Cells can also contain functions, which are pre-built formulas that perform specific calculations using the data in the worksheet.

3. **Editing Cells**: To enter or edit the contents of a cell, simply click on the desired cell and start typing. The formula bar, located above the worksheet grid, displays the contents of the selected cell and allows you to enter or edit formulas, functions, or text. You can also use the F2 key to directly edit the contents of a cell.

4. **Formatting Cells:** Excel provides various formatting options to customize the appearance of cells. You can change the font style, size, and color, apply bold or italic formatting, add borders, align text, and more. Formatting options help make your data more readable and visually appealing.

5. **Cell Names**: Excel allows you to define names for cells or ranges to make it easier to refer to them in formulas or functions. Cell names can be descriptive and meaningful, helping you understand the purpose of the data in the cell and making your formulas more readable.

6. **Cell Merging**: In Excel, you can merge cells to combine multiple cells into a single, larger cell. This is useful, for example, when creating headings or labels that span across several columns or rows. Merged cells can be formatted and centered to create a more organized and visually appealing worksheet.

7. **Cell Protection**: Excel provides the option to protect cells or ranges, preventing accidental changes to critical data. You can lock cells to prevent editing, while allowing users to input data in specific cells or ranges. Cell protection is particularly useful when sharing workbooks with others or when you want to maintain the integrity of your data.

Understanding the concept of cells is essential for effectively working with data in Excel. By utilizing the features and functions available for cells, you can organize and analyze your data efficiently, perform calculations, and present your information in a clear and professional manner.

Understanding Columns in Excel

Columns are one of the fundamental components of Microsoft Excel. They run vertically from top to bottom in the worksheet grid and provide a way to organize and manage data in a structured manner. Understanding columns is crucial for effectively working with data and performing calculations in Excel.

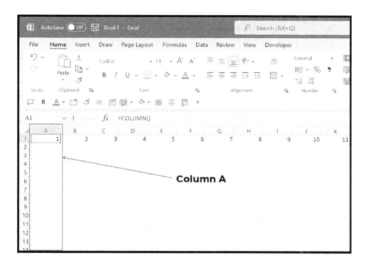

Here are some key points to understand about columns in Excel:

1. **Column Headers:** Each column in Excel is labeled with a letter at the top to provide a reference and identify its position within the worksheet grid. The first column is labeled with the letter "A," the second column with "B," and so on. These column headers facilitate navigation and referencing specific columns in formulas or functions.

2. **Column Width**: Excel allows you to adjust the width of columns to display data properly. You can manually resize columns by dragging the divider between the column headers, or you can use the "AutoFit" feature to automatically adjust column width to fit the content within the cells. Proper column width ensures that data is visible and easily readable.

3. **Sorting and Filtering**: Excel provides powerful sorting and filtering options that can be applied to columns. You can sort data within a column in ascending or descending order based on its values. Filtering allows you to display only specific data in a column based on certain criteria, making it easier to analyze and work with large datasets.

4. **Inserting and Deleting Columns**: Excel allows you to insert or delete columns as needed. Inserting a column shifts the existing columns to the right, making room for the new column. Deleting a column removes it from the worksheet grid and shifts the columns to the left. This flexibility allows for efficient organization and arrangement of data.

5. **Formulas and Functions**: Columns play a vital role in performing calculations in Excel. You can use formulas and functions in columns to derive values based on the data in other columns. By referencing cells or ranges within the same column or across multiple columns, you can perform complex calculations, such as mathematical operations, logical tests, or statistical analyses.

6. **Column Charts and Graphs**: Excel provides various chart types to visualize data, and columns are commonly used as the basis for creating column charts. A column chart represents data using vertical bars of varying heights, where the height of each bar corresponds to the value it represents. Column charts are effective for comparing data across different categories or time periods.

7. **Column Labels and Formatting**: Column labels are used to provide descriptive names or headings for the data within a column. You can format column labels to differentiate them from the rest of the data, such as applying bold or italic styles, changing font colors, or increasing font sizes. Properly labeled and formatted columns enhance data clarity and improve the overall presentation of your worksheet.

Understanding the concept of columns is essential for properly organizing and analyzing data in Excel. By utilizing the features and functions specific to columns, you can efficiently work with your data, perform calculations, and create visual representations that help convey information effectively.

Understanding Rows in Excel

Rows are a fundamental component of Microsoft Excel that run horizontally from left to right in the worksheet grid. They provide a way to organize and manage data in a structured manner. Understanding rows is crucial for effectively working with data and performing calculations in Excel.

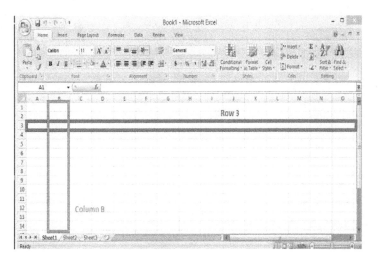

Here are some key points to understand about rows in Excel:

1. **Row Numbers**: Each row in Excel is labeled with a number on the left-hand side to provide a reference and identify its position within the worksheet grid. The first row is labeled with the number "1," the second row with "2," and so on. These row numbers facilitate navigation and referencing specific rows in formulas or functions.

2. **Row Height**: Excel allows you to adjust the height of rows to display data properly. You can manually resize rows by dragging the divider between the row numbers or use the "AutoFit" feature to automatically adjust row height to fit the content within the cells. Proper row height ensures that data is visible and easily readable.

3. **Inserting and Deleting Rows**: Excel allows you to insert or delete rows as needed. Inserting a row shifts the existing rows below it down, making room for the new row. Deleting a row removes it from the worksheet grid and shifts the rows above it up. This flexibility allows for efficient organization and arrangement of data.

4. **Sorting and Filtering:** Excel provides powerful sorting and filtering options that can be applied to rows. You can sort data within a row in ascending or descending order based on its values. Filtering allows you to display only specific data in a row based on certain criteria, making it easier to analyze and work with large datasets.

5. **Formulas and Functions:** Rows play a vital role in performing calculations in Excel. You can use formulas and functions in rows to derive values based on the data in other rows. By referencing cells or ranges within the same row or across multiple rows, you can perform complex calculations, such as mathematical operations, logical tests, or statistical analyses.

6. **Row Labels and Formatting:** Row labels are used to provide descriptive names or headings for the data within a row. You can format row labels to differentiate them from the rest of the data, such as applying bold or italic styles, changing font colors, or increasing font sizes. Properly labeled and formatted rows enhance data clarity and improve the overall presentation of your worksheet.

7. **Data Entry**: Rows are where you enter and organize your data in Excel. Each cell within a row can hold various types of data, such as text, numbers, dates, or formulas. By entering data in a structured manner within specific rows, you can analyze and manipulate it using Excel's built-in functions and features.

Understanding the concept of rows is essential for properly organizing and analyzing data in Excel. By utilizing the features and functions specific to rows, you can efficiently work with your data, perform calculations, and create insightful reports and analyses.

Understanding Ranges in Excel

Ranges are a fundamental concept in Microsoft Excel and play a crucial role in managing and manipulating data. A range in Excel refers to a group of cells, either continuous or non-contiguous, that are selected or referenced together. Understanding ranges is essential for efficiently working with data and performing calculations in Excel.

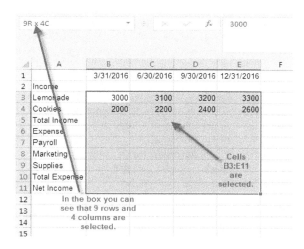

Here are some key points to understand about ranges in Excel:

1. **Selecting a Range:** To work with data in Excel, you need to select a range of cells. You can select a single cell, multiple cells, or an entire range by clicking and dragging your mouse across the desired cells. You can also use keyboard shortcuts or the "Go To" feature to select specific cells or ranges based on criteria such as cell references, column names, or row numbers.

2. **Range References**: Range references refer to a specific range of cells in Excel formulas and functions. A range reference is typically represented by a combination of the starting cell and ending cell, separated by a colon. For example, A1:B5 represents the range of cells from A1 to B5. Range references are used to perform calculations, manipulate data, and create dynamic formulas.

3. **Performing Calculations:** Ranges are essential for performing calculations in Excel. You can use formulas and functions on a range of cells to derive values based on the data within the range. Excel provides a wide range of built-in functions that can be applied to ranges, allowing you to perform mathematical operations, logical tests, statistical analyses, and more.

4. **Range Names**: Excel allows you to assign a name to a range, making it easier to refer to that range in formulas and functions. By assigning a meaningful name to a range, you can enhance the readability and understanding of your formulas. Range names also make it easier to work with large datasets and complex calculations, as you can reference the range name instead of specific cell references.

5. **Modifying Data within a Range**: Ranges provide a convenient way to modify and manipulate data. You can enter or edit data within a range of cells, apply formatting, apply data validation rules, or perform other data manipulation tasks. Modifying data within a range allows you to update and maintain the integrity of your data efficiently.

6. **Sorting and Filtering Ranges**: Excel provides powerful options for sorting and filtering data within a range. Sorting allows you to arrange data in ascending or descending order based on specific criteria, such as alphabetical order or numerical value. Filtering allows you to display only specific data within a range based on certain criteria. Sorting and filtering ranges is particularly useful for analyzing and visualizing data.

7. **Range Operations**: Excel offers various operations and features that can be applied to a range. For example, you can transpose a range to change the orientation of the data from row-wise to column-wise, or vice versa. You can also apply conditional formatting to highlight specific cells within a range based on certain conditions.

Understanding ranges in Excel is crucial for effectively managing and manipulating data. By utilizing the features and functions specific to ranges, you can efficiently work with your data, perform calculations, and create insightful reports and analyses. Ranges provide a structured approach to organizing and analyzing data, making Excel a powerful tool for data management and analysis.

Basic Functions and Formulas

Functions and formulas are essential tools in Microsoft Excel that allow you to perform calculations, manipulate data, and automate tasks. Understanding the basic functions and formulas in Excel is crucial for effectively working with data and creating insightful reports and analyses. Here are some key functions and formulas to understand in Excel:

1. **SUM**: The SUM function is used to add up a range of cells or numbers in Excel. The formula syntax is "=SUM(range)" where "range" represents the cells or numbers you want to add. For example, "=SUM(A1:A5)" would add up the values in cells A1 to A5.

2. **AVERAGE**: The AVERAGE function calculates the average of a range of cells or numbers in Excel. Its formula syntax is "=AVERAGE(range)". For example, "=AVERAGE(B2:B6)" would calculate the average of the values in cells B2 to B6.

3. **COUNT**: The COUNT function counts the number of cells that contain numbers in a range. Its formula syntax is "=COUNT(range)". For example, "=COUNT(C1:C10)" would count the number of cells in the range C1 to C10 that contain numbers.

4. **MIN and MAX**: The MIN and MAX functions are used to find the minimum and maximum values in a range of cells or numbers, respectively. The formulas are "=MIN(range)" and "=MAX(range)". For example, "=MIN(D1:D8)" would find the smallest value in the range D1 to D8.

5. **IF**: The IF function allows you to perform conditional calculations in Excel. Its formula syntax is "=IF(condition, value_if_true, value_if_false)". For example, "=IF(A1>10, "Yes", "No")" would check if the value in cell A1 is greater than 10 and return "Yes" if true, or "No" if false.

6. **CONCATENATE**: The CONCATENATE function is used to join text strings together in Excel. Its formula syntax is "=CONCATENATE(text1, text2, ...)". For example, "=CONCATENATE(A1, " ", B1)" would join the text in cell A1 and a space with the text in cell B1.

7. **VLOOKUP**: The VLOOKUP function is used to search for a value in the leftmost column of a table and return a corresponding value from a specified column. Its formula syntax is "=VLOOKUP(lookup_value, table_array, col_index_num, [range_lookup])". For example, "=VLOOKUP(A2, B2:D10, 3, FALSE)" would search for the value in cell A2 in the range B2 to D10 and return the corresponding value from the third column.

8. **SUMIF**: The SUMIF function adds up values that meet a specific criterion in a range. Its formula syntax is "=SUMIF(range, criteria, [sum_range])". For example, "=SUMIF(A1:A5, ">10")" would sum up the values in the range A1 to A5 that are greater than 10.

These are just a few examples of the basic functions and formulas in Excel. Excel offers a wide range of built-in functions that can be combined and nested together to perform complex calculations and data manipulations. By mastering these basic functions and formulas, you can efficiently work with data, automate tasks, and create powerful analyses in Excel.

Entering Data into Cells

Entering data into cells is one of the fundamental tasks in Microsoft Excel. Each cell in Excel can hold different types of data, including numbers, text, dates, and formulas.

Here are some key points to understand when entering data into cells:

1. **Select the Cell**: Before entering data, you need to select the cell where you want to enter the data. You can simply click on a cell with your mouse or use the arrow keys to navigate to the desired cell.

2. **Type the Data**: Once the cell is selected, you can start typing the data. Depending on the type of data you are entering, Excel will automatically format the cell accordingly. For example, if you enter a number, Excel will align the data to the right side of the cell by default.

3. **Edit the Data**: If you need to make changes to the data, you can simply click on the cell and start editing the contents. You can use the backspace or delete key to remove characters or use the arrow keys to navigate within the text.

4. **Enter Formulas**: Excel allows you to enter formulas into cells to perform calculations. To enter a formula, start by typing an equal sign (=) followed by the formula expression. For example, "=A1+B1" would add the values in cells A1 and B1.

5. **AutoFill**: Excel provides the AutoFill feature, which allows you to quickly populate a series of cells with a pattern or sequence. To use AutoFill, select the cell with the initial value, hover over the bottom right corner of the cell until the fill handle appears, and then click and drag to fill the desired range.

6. **Copy and Paste**: You can also copy and paste data from one cell to another in Excel. To copy data, select the cell with the data, press Ctrl+C, select the target cell, and press Ctrl+V to paste the data. You can also use the Copy and Paste buttons on the Home tab in the Ribbon.

7. **Data Validation**: Excel provides data validation options to control the type of data entered into cells. You can apply data validation rules to restrict inputs to certain formats, such as numbers within a specific range or text that meets certain criteria. This helps maintain data integrity and consistency.

8. **Protecting Cells**: In Excel, you can protect cells to prevent accidental or unauthorized changes to the data. By locking specific cells, you can ensure that only authorized users can modify them. To protect cells, you can use the Protect Sheet or Protect Workbook options under the Review tab in the Ribbon.

Entering data into cells correctly is important to ensure accurate calculations and reporting in Excel. By understanding the basics of entering data, editing contents, using formulas, and using features such as AutoFill and data validation, you can work efficiently with your data and maintain the integrity of your Excel spreadsheets.

Performing Basic Calculations with Formulas

Performing basic calculations with formulas in Excel is a powerful way to automate mathematical operations and save time.

Here are some key points to understand when using formulas for calculations in Excel:

1. **Formula Syntax**: In Excel, a formula always starts with an equal sign (=). The formula consists of cell references, operators, and functions. For example, "=A1+B1" would add the values in cells A1 and B1.

2. **Cell References**: Cell references are used in formulas to specify the cells that contain the data for the calculation. A cell reference consists of the column letter followed by the row number. For example, "A1" refers to the cell in the first column and first row.

3. **Operators**: Excel supports a variety of mathematical operators for calculations, including addition (+), subtraction (-), multiplication (*), division (/), and exponentiation (^). For example, "=A1+B1" would add the values in cells A1 and B1.

4. **Parentheses**: You can use parentheses in formulas to control the order of operations. For example, if you have the formula "=A1+(B1-C1)" and want to subtract C1 from B1 before adding it to A1, you can use parentheses to clarify the calculation.

5. **Functions**: Excel provides a wide range of built-in functions that perform specific calculations. These functions can be used in formulas to simplify complex calculations or perform specialized operations. Functions are usually followed by parentheses containing arguments, which are inputs for the function. For example, "=SUM(A1:A5)" would calculate the sum of the values in cells A1 to A5.

6. **AutoSum**: Excel offers the AutoSum feature, which allows you to quickly calculate sums, averages, counts, and other common functions. To use AutoSum, select the cell below or to the right of the data you want to calculate, click on the AutoSum button in the Home tab, and Excel will automatically create the formula for you.

7. **Relative and Absolute Cell** References: By default, cell references in formulas are relative, meaning they can change as the formula is copied to different cells. However, you can use absolute cell references with the dollar sign ($) to fix a reference to a specific cell. For example, "A1" would always refer to cell A1, even if the formula is copied to other cells.

8. **Error Handling**: If a formula contains errors, such as a circular reference or a division by zero, Excel will display an error message. You can use error handling techniques, such as the IFERROR function, to handle these errors gracefully and display custom messages or alternative calculations.

By using formulas effectively in Excel, you can perform basic calculations, such as addition, subtraction, multiplication, and division, as well as more complex calculations using functions and operators. Remember to double-check your formulas for accuracy and use appropriate cell references and operators to yield the desired results.

Using Functions such as SUM, AVERAGE, MAX, and MIN

Here are some commonly used functions in Excel:

1. **SUM:** The SUM function adds up a range of cells. To use it, simply enter "=SUM(" followed by the range of cells you want to add up, enclosed in parentheses. For example, "=SUM(A1:A5)" would add up the values in cells A1 to A5.

2. **AVERAGE**: The AVERAGE function calculates the average of a range of cells. To use it, enter "=AVERAGE(" followed by the range of cells you want to average. For example, "=AVERAGE(A1:A5)" would calculate the average of the values in cells A1 to A5.

3. **MAX**: The MAX function returns the largest value in a range of cells. To use it, enter "=MAX(" followed by the range of cells you want to find the maximum value from. For example, "=MAX(A1:A5)" would return the largest value in cells A1 to A5.

4. **MIN**: The MIN function returns the smallest value in a range of cells. To use it, enter "=MIN(" followed by the range of cells you want to find the minimum value from. For example, "=MIN(A1:A5)" would return the smallest value in cells A1 to A5.

These functions can be combined with other functions and operators to perform more complex calculations. For example, you can use the SUM function within an AVERAGE function to calculate the average of a subset of values.

Remember, when using functions, you need to enclose the range of cells in parentheses, and separate multiple cells or ranges with commas. You can also use absolute or relative cell references for the range of cells, depending on whether you want the range to change when copied or not.

Applying Relative and Absolute Cell References

Relative and absolute cell references are essential when working with formulas in Excel. They allow you to control how cell references behave when a formula is copied or filled to other cells.

Here's an explanation of relative and absolute cell references:

Relative Cell References: By default, cell references in formulas are relative. This means that when you copy a formula to another cell, the references adjust automatically based on their relative position to the new location. For example, if you have a formula "=A1+B1" in cell C1 and you copy it to cell C2, the formula will automatically adjust to "=A2+B2" because the references have moved down by one row.

Absolute Cell References: Sometimes you may want to lock in a specific cell reference so that it doesn't change when you copy a formula. You can do this by using absolute cell references. To create an absolute reference, use the dollar sign ($) before the column letter and/or the row number. For example, "A1" refers to cell A1, and both the column and the row are fixed.

- **Absolute Column Reference**: If you want to keep the column reference constant while allowing the row reference to adjust, use a dollar sign before the column letter. For example, "=$A1" would lock in column A while the row adjusts when copied.
- **Absolute Row Reference**: If you want to fix the row reference while allowing the column reference to change, use a dollar sign before the row number. For example, "=A$1" would maintain row 1 while the column adjusts.

Mixed Cell References: You can also create mixed cell references, where one part is absolute and another part is relative. For example, "$A1" would keep column A constant while allowing the row to adjust when copied.

To apply absolute or mixed cell references in a formula, simply type the dollar signs ($) in front of the appropriate column letters and/or row numbers. You can also use the F4 key as a shortcut to toggle between different types of references when editing a formula.

Using relative, absolute, or mixed cell references allows you to control how formulas behave when copied or filled to other cells. By leveraging these references, you can perform calculations on different cells while maintaining the desired references and producing accurate results in Excel.

Formatting and Customizing Worksheets

Formatting and customizing worksheets in Excel is essential for creating professional-looking and easy-to-read spreadsheets.

Here are some key tips and techniques for formatting and customizing worksheets:

1. **Adjusting Column Width and Row Height**: You can resize columns and rows to fit the contents of your cells. Double-click the right boundary of a column header or the bottom boundary of a row header to automatically adjust the width or height to best fit the content.
2. **Changing Font Styles and Sizes**: Modify font styles and sizes to enhance readability or match specific formatting requirements. Select the cells or range of cells you want to format, go to the "Home" tab, and use the various font options available in the "Font" group, such as font type, size, bold, italic, and more.
3. **Applying Cell Borders**: Use borders to create separation between cells or highlight specific regions of your worksheet. Select the cells or range of cells, go to the "Home" tab, and choose the borders option from the "Font" group. You can select different border styles, thickness, and colors.
4. **Adding Cell Fill Colors**: Apply fill colors to cells to make them stand out or indicate different categories. Select the cells or range of cells, go to the "Home" tab, and choose a fill color from the "Font" group. You can also use the "Fill Color" button in the "Format Cells" dialog box to select more advanced fill options.
5. **Formatting Numbers and Dates**: Format numbers and dates to display in a specific format, such as currency, percentage, or date formats. Select the cells or range of cells, right-click, choose "Format Cells," and select the desired number or date format from the "Number" tab.
6. **Merging and Centering Cells**: Merge multiple cells into a single cell and center the contents for better presentation. Select the cells you want to merge, right-click, choose "Format Cells," and go to the "Alignment" tab. Check the "Merge cells" option and select the desired horizontal and vertical alignment.

7. **Using Conditional Formatting**: Apply conditional formatting to highlight cells based on specific conditions. Select the cells or range of cells, go to the "Home" tab, and choose the "Conditional Formatting" option in the "Styles" group. From there, select the desired formatting rule and customize the conditions and formatting options accordingly.

8. **Filtering and Sorting** Data: Filter and sort data to organize and analyze information more effectively. Select the range of data, go to the "Data" tab, and use the "Sort" and "Filter" buttons to sort and filter the data based on specific criteria.

9. **Adding Headers and Footers**: Include headers and footers to add titles, page numbers, or other information to your worksheets when printing. Go to the "Insert" tab, click on the "Header & Footer" button, and select the desired options from the available options in the header and footer section.

10. **Customizing Page Setup**: Adjust the page orientation, margins, paper size, and other printing settings by going to the "Page Layout" tab and using the "Page Setup" group options. You can also set print areas and page breaks from this tab.

By utilizing these formatting and customization features, you can improve the appearance and organization of your Excel worksheets, making them more visually appealing and easier to navigate.

Formatting cells, fonts, and numbers

When working with Microsoft Excel, it is important to format cells, fonts, and numbers to make your worksheets more visually appealing and easier to read.

Here are some tips for formatting these elements:

Formatting Cells:

1. Select the cells or range of cells you want to format.

2. Right-click on the selection and choose "Format Cells" from the context menu, or go to the "Home" tab and click on the "Format" button in the "Cells" group.

3. In the "Number" tab of the "Format Cells" dialog box, choose the desired category for your data, such as "General", "Number", "Currency", "Percentage", "Date", or "Time".

4. Pick a formatting option within the category, or customize it further by adjusting the decimal places, symbol placement, and other settings.

5. Click "OK" to apply the formatting to the selected cells.

Formatting Fonts:

1. Select the cells or range of cells you want to format.

2. Go to the "Home" tab and use the options in the "Font" group to change the font type, font size, font color, and style (bold, italic, underline, etc.).

3. You can also access additional font formatting options by clicking on the "Dialog Box Launcher" button in the bottom right corner of the "Font" group.

4. Once you have made your desired changes, the formatting will be applied to the selected cells.

Formatting Numbers:

1. Select the cells or range of cells containing the numbers you want to format.

2. Go to the "Home" tab and use the options in the "Number" group to adjust the number formatting.

3. You can choose from common number formats like "Currency", "Percentage", or "Number", or click on the "More Number Formats" option to access additional formatting options.

4. In the "Format Cells" dialog box that appears, you can customize the formatting further by specifying the number of decimal places, thousand separators, and other settings.

5. Click "OK" to apply the number formatting to the selected cells.

Remember to regularly review and update formatting as needed to maintain consistency and clarity in your Excel worksheets.

Applying conditional formatting

Conditional formatting in Excel allows you to apply formatting to cells based on certain conditions or criteria. This feature makes it easier to highlight important or relevant data and visually analyze your worksheets.

Here's how you can apply conditional formatting in Excel:

1. Select the cells or range of cells that you want to apply conditional formatting to.

2. Go to the "Home" tab and click on the "Conditional Formatting" button in the "Styles" group.

3. From the dropdown menu, choose the type of conditional formatting you want to apply. Excel offers various pre-defined rules, such as "Highlight Cells Rules", "Top/Bottom Rules", "Data Bars", "Color Scales", and "Icon Sets".

4. Select the specific rule or format option you want to apply. For example, if you choose "Highlight Cells Rules", you can then select from options like "Greater Than", "Less Than", "Between", "Duplicate Values", "Text that Contains", etc.

5. A dialog box will appear, allowing you to set the conditions and formatting for the selected cells. Enter the criteria, values, or formulas that need to be met for the formatting to be applied.

6. Customize the formatting of the cells by choosing the font, fill color, borders, and other formatting options.

7. Click "OK" to apply the conditional formatting to the selected cells.

However, note:

1. You can also add multiple conditional formatting rules to a single set of cells by repeating the process.

2. Remember that you can always modify or remove conditional formatting by selecting the cells and going back to the "Conditional Formatting" menu to edit or delete the rules.

3. Conditional formatting can greatly enhance the visual analysis of your data in Excel and help you quickly identify trends, outliers, or specific values that meet certain criteria.

Creating and Modifying Cell Styles

In Microsoft Excel, cell styles provide an efficient way to apply consistent formatting across multiple cells, making your worksheets look more professional and organized.

Here's how you can create and modify cell styles in Excel:

Creating a Cell Style:

1. Select a cell that has the desired formatting you want to save as a cell style.

2. Go to the "Home" tab and click on the "Cell Styles" button, which is in the "Styles" group. Alternatively, you can use the keyboard shortcut "Ctrl+Shift+S" to open the "Cell Styles" dialog box.

3. In the "Cell Styles" dialog box, click on the "New Cell Style" button at the bottom left corner.

4. In the "Style name" field, provide a unique name for your new cell style.

5. Customize the formatting options for your cell style by navigating through the tabs in the "Format" section. You can modify font, border, alignment, number format, fill color, and more.

6. Once you've made all the desired formatting changes, click "OK" to create the new cell style.

Applying a Cell Style:

1. Select the cells or range of cells that you want to apply a cell style to.

2. Open the "Cell Styles" dialog box by clicking on the "Cell Styles" button on the "Home" tab, or using the keyboard shortcut "Ctrl+Shift+S".

3. Locate the desired cell style in the "Cell Styles" dialog box.

4. Double-click on the cell style to apply it to the selected cells. Alternatively, you can right-click on the cell style and choose "Apply" from the context menu.

Modifying a Cell Style:

1. Go to the "Home" tab and click on the "Cell Styles" button, or use the shortcut "Ctrl+Shift+S", to open the "Cell Styles" dialog box.

2. In the "Cell Styles" dialog box, locate the cell style you want to modify.

3. Right-click on the cell style and choose "Modify" from the context menu, or select the cell style and click the "Modify" button at the bottom.

4. In the "Modify Style" dialog box, make the necessary changes to the formatting options.

5. Click "OK" to save the modified cell style.

You can also delete a cell style by selecting it in the "Cell Styles" dialog box and clicking the "Delete" button.

By creating and modifying cell styles in Excel, you can easily apply consistent formatting to cells throughout your worksheets, saving time and ensuring a professional and organized look.

Inserting and Formatting Tables and Graphics

Inserting and formatting tables and graphics in Microsoft Excel can enhance the visual appeal and organization of your data.

Here's a step-by-step guide on how to insert and format tables and graphics in Excel:

Inserting a Table:

1. Open your Excel worksheet and select the range of cells that you want to convert into a table.

2. Go to the "Insert" tab and click on the "Table" button in the "Tables" group. Alternatively, you can use the shortcut "Ctrl+T".

3. In the "Create Table" dialog box, verify that the correct range is selected in the "Where is the data for your table?" field and click "OK".

4. Excel will apply formatting and automatically add a header row to your table. You can customize the table by adding or removing rows and columns and modifying the table style using the options available in the "Table Design" tab.

Formatting a Table:

1. With the table selected, go to the "Table Design" tab, which appears automatically when you insert a table.

2. In the "Table Styles" group, you can choose from a variety of predefined table styles to apply to your table. Simply click on the desired style to see a preview, and then click on it again to apply it.

3. Customize the formatting of your table by using the formatting options in the "Table Styles Options" group. You can change the table header, total row, banded rows, first column, and last column formatting.

4. Apply additional formatting options, such as changing font styles, colors, cell borders, and background colors, using the options available in the "Home" tab.

Inserting Graphics:

1. Select the cell or range of cells where you want to insert a graphic.

2. Go to the "Insert" tab and select the type of graphic you want to insert. For example, you can choose to insert a picture from a file, a shape, a SmartArt graphic, or a chart.

3. Follow the on-screen instructions to insert the specific graphic type. For example, if you choose to insert a picture, you will need to browse for the image file on your computer and select it.

4. Resize and position the graphic as desired by dragging its corners or edges.

Formatting Graphics:

1. With the graphic selected, go to the "Format" tab that appears when a graphic is inserted.

2. In the "Picture Styles" group, you can choose from various predefined picture styles or apply individual formatting options such as picture effects, picture borders, and picture layouts.

3. Customize additional formatting options, such as adjusting the brightness, contrast, and color of the graphic, by using the options available in the "Adjust" group.

4. Apply other formatting options, such as changing the shape outline, fill color, and effects, using the options available in the "Shape Styles" group.

By inserting and formatting tables and graphics in Excel, you can present your data in a visually appealing and organized manner. This makes it easier for others to understand and interpret the information in your worksheets.

Data Management and Analysis

Data management and analysis are essential tasks in Excel, as they allow you to organize and analyze large amounts of data efficiently.

Here are some key aspects of data management and analysis in Excel:

1. **Data Entry:** Excel provides a user-friendly interface for entering data into spreadsheets. You can input data manually or import it from external sources, such as databases or text files.

2. **Data Cleaning**: Before performing any analysis, it's important to clean and prepare your data. Excel offers various tools and functions for cleaning data, such as removing duplicates, correcting formatting errors, and handling missing values.

3. **Sorting and Filtering**: Excel allows you to sort your data in ascending or descending order based on one or multiple columns. Filtering enables you to display specific data based on certain criteria, allowing you to focus on subsets of your data for analysis.

4. **Formulas and Functions**: Excel provides a wide range of built-in functions and formulas that allow you to perform calculations and data manipulations. Functions such as SUM, AVERAGE, COUNT, and IF are commonly used for data analysis.

5. **PivotTables**: PivotTables are powerful tools in Excel for summarizing and analyzing large datasets. They allow you to quickly generate summary reports by arranging and summarizing data based on different criteria. PivotTables also enable you to create calculated fields and apply filters to further analyze your data.

6. **Charts and Graphs**: Excel offers a variety of chart types that allow you to visualize your data. By creating charts and graphs, you can identify trends, patterns, and relationships in your data, making it easier to interpret and present your findings.

7. **Data Analysis Tools**: Excel provides various data analysis tools, such as regression analysis, data tables, goal seek, and scenario manager. These tools enable you to perform advanced analysis and make data-driven decisions.

8. **Data Validation**: Excel allows you to set validation rules to ensure data accuracy and consistency. You can restrict data entry to specific formats or ranges, preventing errors and ensuring the integrity of your data.

9. **Data Consolidation**: If you need to combine data from multiple worksheets or workbooks, Excel's data consolidation feature allows you to merge data from different sources into a single consolidated dataset for further analysis.

10. **Macros and Visual Basic for Applications (VBA)**: Advanced users can automate data management and analysis tasks using Excel's macro recorder or by writing VBA code. This allows for increased efficiency and customizability in data processing and analysis.

By utilizing these features and techniques in Excel, you can effectively manage and analyze your data, allowing you to gain valuable insights and make informed decisions.

Sorting and Filtering Data

Sorting and filtering data are essential tasks in Excel that allow you to organize and analyze your data more effectively.

Here's a closer look at sorting and filtering in Excel:

Sorting Data:
Sorting data in Excel involves arranging the data in a specific order based on the values in one or more columns. This is useful for identifying patterns, finding specific values, or organizing the data for further analysis.

To sort data in Excel:

1. Select the range of cells you want to sort.

2. Go to the Data tab on the Excel ribbon.

3. Click on the Sort button or choose the Sort option from the drop-down menu.

4. In the Sort dialog box, specify the column to sort by and choose whether to sort in ascending or descending order.

5. Click OK to perform the sort operation.

Excel offers additional options for sorting, such as sorting by multiple columns, sorting by cell color or font color, or sorting by custom lists.

Filtering Data:

Filtering data in Excel allows you to display only the specific rows that meet certain criteria, hiding the rest of the data temporarily. This is useful for narrowing down data sets and focusing on specific subsets of data for analysis or reporting.

To filter data in Excel:

1. Select the range of cells you want to filter.

2. Go to the Data tab on the Excel ribbon.

3. Click on the Filter button or choose the Filter option from the drop-down menu.

4. Excel will add filter arrows to the header row of each column in the selected range.

5. Click on the filter arrow for a specific column and choose the desired criteria to filter by (e.g., text filters, number filters, date filters, etc.).

6. Excel will hide any rows that do not meet the selected filter criteria.

You can apply multiple filters to different columns simultaneously, allowing for more complex data analysis. You can also use custom filters to specify specific criteria or use advanced filter options for more advanced filtering scenarios.

Sorting and filtering data in Excel greatly enhances data analysis by enabling you to identify trends, patterns, and outliers quickly. Whether you need to sort your data for presentation or filter your data to focus on specific subsets, Excel provides powerful tools to help you manage and analyze your data effectively.

Using Data Validation to Control Input

Using data validation in Excel allows you to control and restrict the type of data that can be entered into cells. This is useful for ensuring data accuracy, maintaining consistency, and reducing errors in your spreadsheets.

Here's a closer look at how to use data validation in Excel to control input:

1. Select the cells where you want to apply data validation.

2. Go to the Data tab on the Excel ribbon.

3. Click on the Data Validation button or choose the Data Validation option from the drop-down menu.

4. In the Data Validation dialog box, choose the type of validation you want to apply. There are various types of validation you can use, such as whole numbers, decimal numbers, dates, text lengths, custom formulas, and more.

5. Configure the validation criteria based on your requirements. For example, if you want to allow only whole numbers between 1 and 10, choose "Whole number" as the validation type and set the minimum and maximum values accordingly.

6. You can also provide an input message to guide users on what type of data is expected in the cell.

7. Optionally, you can add an error alert to display a message when users enter invalid data. You can customize the error message and choose the style of the error alert (e.g., stop, warning, or information).

8. Click OK to apply the data validation to the selected cells.

Once data validation is applied, Excel will enforce the validation criteria, and users will only be able to enter data that meets the specified conditions. If users attempt to enter invalid data, Excel will display the error alert and prevent the entry.

Data validation is a powerful tool that helps ensure data integrity and accuracy in Excel. It enables you to control and restrict data input, reducing errors and inconsistencies. By setting up data validation rules, you can enhance the quality and reliability of your spreadsheets.

Creating and modifying pivot tables

Creating and modifying pivot tables in Excel allows you to summarize and analyze large amounts of data quickly and easily. Pivot tables provide a flexible way to organize and manipulate data, allowing you to generate meaningful insights from your data.

Here's a step-by-step guide on creating and modifying pivot tables in Excel:

Creating a Pivot Table:

1. Select the range of data you want to analyze.

2. Go to the Insert tab on the Excel ribbon.

3. Click on the PivotTable button or choose the PivotTable option from the drop-down menu.

4. In the Create PivotTable dialog box, verify that the selected range of data is correct.

5. Choose where you want to place the pivot table: on a new worksheet or in an existing worksheet.

6. Click OK to create the pivot table.

7. By default, Excel will create a blank pivot table with the PivotTable Field List panel on the right side of the screen.

Modifying a Pivot Table:

1. Use the PivotTable Field List to add fields to your pivot table. Drag and drop fields from the Field List into the Rows, Columns, or Values area to determine how the data is summarized.

2. To change the summary operation, click on the drop-down arrow in the Values area and select the desired summary function (e.g., Sum, Count, Average, etc.).

3. To filter the data, drag a field into the Filters area and choose the desired criteria for filtering.

4. To change the ordering of the fields in your pivot table, simply drag and drop them within the Rows or Columns area.

5. You can also format your pivot table by applying different styles, customizing the layout, or adding conditional formatting.

6. Pivot tables offer various additional options and features, such as calculated fields, grouping data, sorting, filtering, and more. You can access these options by right-clicking within your pivot table or using the PivotTable Analyze or Design tabs on the Excel ribbon.

When you modify a pivot table, Excel automatically updates the summary and analysis based on your changes. This dynamic nature of pivot tables allows you to explore and analyze your data from different perspectives without the need for manual calculations or adjustments.

Pivot tables are an essential tool for data analysis in Excel, providing a flexible and efficient way to summarize and manipulate large datasets. By creating and modifying pivot tables, you can gain valuable insights and make informed decisions based on your data.

Performing what-if analysis with scenarios and goal seek

Performing what-if analysis with scenarios and goal seek in Excel allows you to explore different scenarios and determine the impact of changing variables on your data. What-if analysis helps you make informed decisions and plan for different possibilities.

Here's a step-by-step guide on performing what-if analysis with scenarios and goal seek in Excel:

Scenarios:

1. Start by organizing your data in a worksheet, with different variables and their corresponding outcomes or results.

2. Go to the Data tab on the Excel ribbon and choose the What-If Analysis option.

3. Select the Scenario Manager from the drop-down menu.

4. In the Scenario Manager dialog box, click on the Add button to create a new scenario.

5. Enter a name for the scenario and specify the cells or ranges that contain the variable values for that scenario.

6. Click OK to save the scenario

7. Repeat the process to add multiple scenarios with different variable values.

8. Once you have added scenarios, you can go back to the Scenario Manager dialog box to view, edit, or delete scenarios as needed.
9. To see the results of each scenario, use the Scenario Summary report, which shows a summary of all the scenarios and their corresponding outcomes.

10. You can also use the Goal Seek feature in scenarios to determine the input value required to achieve a desired outcome or result.

Goal Seek:

1. Start by identifying the desired outcome or result you want to achieve by changing a specific input value.

2. Go to the Data tab on the Excel ribbon and choose the What-If Analysis option.

3. Select the Goal Seek option from the drop-down menu.

4. In the Goal Seek dialog box, specify the cell containing the desired outcome, the cell containing the input value that needs to be changed, and the desired value of the outcome.

5. Click OK to run the Goal Seek analysis.

6. Excel will automatically calculate and determine the required input value to achieve the desired outcome.

7. You can also use the Solver add-in in Excel for more complex what-if analysis and optimization problems.

Performing what-if analysis with scenarios and goal seek in Excel allows you to explore different possibilities, understand the impact of changing variables, and make informed decisions. It helps you analyze and plan for various scenarios and determine the best course of action based on your data.

Advanced Formulas and Functions

Advanced formulas and functions in Excel allow you to perform complex calculations and manipulate data with ease. These formulas and functions can help you save time and automate tasks in your spreadsheets.

Here are some common advanced formulas and functions in Excel:

1. **VLOOKUP**:

- The VLOOKUP function is used to search for a value in the first column of a table and then return a corresponding value from a different column in the same row.

- It has four arguments: lookup value, table range, column index number, and an optional range lookup parameter.

- VLOOKUP is commonly used for tasks like searching for employee information based on an employee ID or finding product prices from a product catalog.

2. **INDEX and MATCH:**

- The INDEX and MATCH functions are used together to return a value from a range based on matching criteria.

- INDEX returns the value in a specified cell of a given range, and MATCH searches for a specified value in a range and returns the relative position of that value.

- By combining INDEX and MATCH, you can perform more flexible and versatile lookups in your spreadsheets.

3. **SUMIFS, COUNTIFS, and AVERAGEIFS**:

- These functions allow you to perform conditional summing, counting, and averaging based on multiple criteria.

- SUMIFS adds up values in a range that meet multiple specified criteria.

- COUNTIFS counts the number of cells in a range that meet multiple criteria.

- AVERAGEIFS calculates the average of cells in a range that meet multiple criteria.

- These functions are particularly useful when working with large datasets and you want to analyze specific subsets of data.

4. **IFERROR**:

- The IFERROR function allows you to handle errors in your formulas and display custom messages or values instead.

- It has two arguments: the formula or expression you want to evaluate and the value or message to display if the formula results in an error.

- IFERROR helps you make your spreadsheets more robust by handling errors gracefully and providing users with meaningful error messages.

5. **CONCATENATE and TEXTJOIN**:

- The CONCATENATE function is used to combine two or more text strings into one.

- TEXTJOIN is similar, but it allows you to combine multiple text strings with a specified delimiter in between.

- These functions are handy for tasks like merging cells, creating custom labels, or formatting data.

These are just a few examples of advanced formulas and functions in Excel. Excel offers a wide range of functions that can help you analyze and manipulate data in sophisticated ways. By mastering these formulas and functions, you can become more efficient and effective in your spreadsheet tasks.

Working with logical and text functions

Working with logical and text functions in Excel can help you manipulate, analyze and extract meaningful information from your data. These functions allow you to perform operations based on logical conditions and manipulate text strings to suit your needs.

Here are some commonly used logical and text functions in Excel:

1. **IF function**:

- The IF function allows you to perform a test and return different values based on the result.

- It has three arguments: the logical test, the value to return if the test is TRUE, and the value to return if the test is FALSE.

- IF is useful for creating conditional formulas, such as calculating a bonus if a sales target is met or determining if a student has passed or failed an exam based on their score.

2. **AND and OR functions**:

- The AND function returns TRUE if all the conditions specified are TRUE, and FALSE otherwise.

- The OR function returns TRUE if at least one of the conditions specified is TRUE, and FALSE otherwise.

- AND and OR are useful for evaluating multiple conditions and making decisions based on the results.

3. **NOT function**:

- The NOT function returns the opposite value of a logical expression.

- It has one argument, which is the logical expression to evaluate.

- NOT is handy for negating a condition or reversing the result of a logical test.

4. **CONCATENATE function**:

- The CONCATENATE function allows you to combine two or more text strings into one.

- It has multiple arguments, which are the text strings you want to combine.

- CONCATENATE is useful for joining names, addresses, or any other text strings within your workbook.

5. **LEFT, RIGHT, and MID functions:**

- The LEFT function returns a specified number of characters from the beginning of a text string.

- The RIGHT function returns a specified number of characters from the end of a text string.

- The MID function returns a specified number of characters from any position within a text string.

- LEFT, RIGHT, and MID are helpful for extracting specific portions of text from cells, such as extracting first names from full names or grabbing particular digits from larger numbers.

6. **LEN function**:

- The LEN function returns the number of characters in a text string.

- It has one argument, which is the text string you want to measure.

- LEN is useful for validating the length of input or determining the size of text strings.

These logical and text functions in Excel can help you manipulate and analyze your data more effectively. By using these functions, you can make your formulas more dynamic, extract relevant information from text strings, and perform logical operations to make decisions based on conditions.

Using lookup functions, such as VLOOKUP and HLOOKUP

Using lookup functions in Excel, such as VLOOKUP and HLOOKUP, can help you find specific values in a table or range and retrieve corresponding data. These functions are commonly used to search for information based on a key or identifier.

Here's how you can use VLOOKUP and HLOOKUP effectively in Excel:

VLOOKUP function:

- The VLOOKUP function searches for a value in the leftmost column of a table and returns a value from a specified column in the same row.

- Its syntax is: =VLOOKUP(lookup_value, table_range, column_index, [range_lookup])

- lookup_value: The value you want to search for.

- table_range: The range of cells that contains the lookup table, including the column that contains the lookup value and the column you want to retrieve the data from.

- column_index: The index number of the column from which you want to retrieve data (1 for the first column, 2 for the second column, and so on).

- range_lookup: An optional parameter that specifies whether you want an exact match or an approximate match. Use FALSE for exact match and TRUE or omitted for approximate match.

Example: =VLOOKUP(A2, B2:E10, 3, FALSE)

This formula searches for the value in cell A2 in the range B2:E10, and returns the corresponding value from the third column of that range.

HLOOKUP function:

- The HLOOKUP function works similar to VLOOKUP, but instead of searching in the leftmost column, it searches in the top row of a table and retrieves data from a specified row.

- Its syntax is: =HLOOKUP(lookup_value, table_range, row_index, [range_lookup])

- lookup_value: The value you want to search for.

- table_range: The range of cells that contains the lookup table, including the top row that contains the lookup value and the row you want to retrieve the data from.

- row_index: The index number of the row from which you want to retrieve data (1 for the first row, 2 for the second row, and so on).

- range_lookup: An optional parameter that specifies whether you want an exact match or an approximate match. Use FALSE for exact match and TRUE or omitted for approximate match.

Example: =HLOOKUP(A2, B2:E10, 2, FALSE)

This formula searches for the value in cell A2 in the range B2:E10 in the top row, and returns the corresponding value from the second row of that range.

VLOOKUP and HLOOKUP functions are useful when you need to retrieve specific information from a table or range based on a key or identifier. They can save you time and make your data analysis and reporting more efficient.

Understanding Array Formulas

Understanding array formulas allows you to perform complex calculations and manipulate multiple values in Excel. An array formula, also known as a CSE (Ctrl + Shift + Enter) formula, is a formula that operates on multiple values at once, rather than just one value.

Here's what you need to know about array formulas in Excel:

Basics of array formulas:

1. Array formulas perform calculations or operations on arrays of data.

2. Arrays are a collection of values arranged in rows and columns.

3. Array formulas allow you to perform calculations across multiple cells or ranges and return multiple results.

Entering array formulas:

1. To enter an array formula, you need to press Ctrl + Shift + Enter instead of just pressing Enter after typing the formula.

2. Excel adds curly braces {} around the formula to indicate that it is an array formula.

3. You cannot manually type the curly braces; Excel automatically adds them when you enter the formula correctly.

How array formulas work:

1. Array formulas perform calculations element by element within arrays.

2. They can perform calculations on a single cell, multiple cells, or ranges of cells.

3. Array formulas can return multiple results, which can be displayed in a contiguous range of cells.

4. Array formulas can be used for calculations like summation, multiplication, comparison, and statistical operations.

Benefits of array formulas:

1. Array formulas save time, as they can perform calculations on multiple values in a single formula.

2. They can handle complex calculations and manipulate large sets of data.

3. Array formulas eliminate the need for intermediate calculations using helper columns or rows.

4. They make it easier to perform calculations with conditional logic across multiple cells or ranges.

Examples of array formulas:

1. SUMPRODUCT: This array formula multiplies corresponding values in two or more arrays and returns the sum of those products.

2. TRANSPOSE: This array formula rotates the values in a range from horizontal to vertical, or vice versa.

3. AVERAGE(IF): This array formula calculates the average of a range of values based on certain conditions.

4. INDEX/MATCH: This array formula combines the INDEX and MATCH functions to retrieve values from a table based on multiple criteria.

Understanding array formulas can greatly enhance your ability to work with complex data sets and perform calculations efficiently in Excel. By mastering array formulas, you can leverage the full power of Excel's array processing capabilities and improve your data analysis and reporting workflows.

Creating and Modifying Nested Formulas

Creating and modifying nested formulas in Excel allows you to perform complex calculations by combining multiple functions together. A nested formula is a formula that contains one or more functions within it.

Here's what you need to know about creating and modifying nested formulas in Excel:

Basic structure of a nested formula:

1. A nested formula consists of a main function, which contains one or more auxiliary functions.

2. The result of the auxiliary function(s) is used as an argument(s) for the main function.

3. Each function within the nested formula must be separated by commas and enclosed within parentheses.

Creating a nested formula:

1. To create a nested formula, start by selecting the cell where you want the result to appear.

2. Begin by typing the equal sign (=) to start the formula.

3. Then, enter the main function followed by an opening parenthesis.

4. Inside the opening parenthesis, enter the auxiliary function(s) separated by commas.

5. Close each function's parentheses properly and then close the main function's parentheses.

6. Press Enter to complete the formula.

Modifying a nested formula:

1. To modify a nested formula, select the cell containing the formula you want to change.

2. Click in the formula bar at the top of the Excel window to edit the formula.

3. Make the necessary modifications to the auxiliary function(s) or add/remove auxiliary functions.

4. Ensure that you maintain the proper structure of the formula by adding or removing parentheses as necessary.

5. Press Enter to save the changes and update the formula result.

Best practices for creating and modifying nested formulas:

1. Break down complex calculations into smaller, manageable steps using auxiliary functions within your nested formula.

2. Use indentation and line breaks to improve readability and clarity of the nested formula.

3. Avoid making the nested formula too long or convoluted, as it can be difficult to debug or understand later.

4. Test the formula with different data sets to ensure it's functioning correctly.

5. Use the Formula Auditing tools in Excel, such as Evaluate Formula, to step through the formula and identify any errors.

Creating and modifying nested formulas in Excel allows you to perform advanced calculations by combining multiple functions.

Data Visualization

Data visualization is the graphical representation of data and information. It utilizes visual elements such as charts, graphs, maps, and diagrams to present data in a clear and understandable way.

Here are some key points to know about data visualization:

Purpose of data visualization:

1. Data visualization aims to communicate data and information visually, enabling easier comprehension and analysis.

2. It helps identify patterns, trends, and relationships in data that may not be immediately apparent in raw form.

3. Visualizing data can enhance decision-making, support storytelling, and assist in conveying complex ideas or concepts.

Benefits of data visualization:

1. Simplifies complex data: Visualizing data allows for a simplified representation of complex datasets, making it easier to grasp and interpret.

2. Enhances insights: Visualization can quickly reveal insights and patterns, enabling users to make data-driven decisions more efficiently.

3. Improves understanding: Visual elements aid in understanding large amounts of data and improve data comprehension for a wider audience.

4. Supports storytelling: Data visualizations can be powerful tools for telling stories and conveying information in a compelling and engaging way.

Types of data visualizations:

1. **Charts and graphs**: Bar charts, line charts, pie charts, scatter plots, and histograms are commonly used to represent numerical data.

2. **Maps**: Geographic visualizations that use maps to display data based on location, such as choropleth maps or heatmaps.

3. **Infographics**: Visual representations that combine text, images, and data to present information succinctly and attractively.

4. **Dashboards**: Interactive displays that provide an overview of multiple visuals and allow users to explore data in real-time.

Considerations for effective data visualization:

1. Choose appropriate visualizations for the type of data being presented and the insights you want to convey.

2. Keep designs simple and uncluttered, avoiding excessive decorations or unnecessary elements that can distract from the data.

3. Use color and contrast effectively to highlight key information and facilitate comparison.

4. Provide clear labels, titles, and legends to ensure the audience understands the data and can interpret the visualization accurately.

5. Make visualizations interactive when possible, allowing users to explore the data and drill down into specific details.

In summary, data visualization is an essential tool for analyzing and understanding data. By presenting data in visual form, it simplifies complex information, enhances insights, and supports effective decision-making. With the wide range of visualization options available, it is important to choose the appropriate type of visualization that best represents your data and effectively communicates your message.

Creating Charts and Graphs

Creating charts and graphs is an important aspect of data visualization.
Here are some steps to consider when creating charts and graphs:

1. **Determine the purpose and message**: Before creating a chart or graph, it's crucial to define the purpose of the visualization and the main message you want to convey. Identify the key insights or trends you want to highlight from your data.

2. **Select the appropriate chart type**: Depending on the nature of your data and the insights you want to present, choose the most suitable chart or graph type. Common types include bar charts, line charts, pie charts, scatter plots, and histograms. Each chart type has its own strengths and weaknesses, so consider the data variables you want to display and the relationships you want to show.

3. **Organize and format your data**: Ensure your data is well-structured and organized for easy chart creation. If needed, perform any necessary data transformations or calculations beforehand. Make sure you have the appropriate data labels and variables for each data point.

4. **Choose a visualization tool or software**: There are many tools and software available for creating charts and graphs, ranging from basic spreadsheet applications to dedicated data visualization software. Some popular options include Microsoft Excel, Tableau, Google Charts, and Python libraries like Matplotlib or Seaborn.

5. **Input and create your chart**: Once you have your data and preferred tool or software, input your data points and select the appropriate chart type. Follow the step-by-step instructions provided by the software or tool to create your chart. Most applications offer customization options for colors, labels, axes, and other visual elements.

6. **Format and enhance your chart:** After creating the basic chart, refine and enhance it to effectively convey your message. Ensure the chart has clear titles, axes labels, legends, and a suitable color scheme that assists in understanding the data. Remove any unnecessary clutter or distractions to keep the chart clean and focused.

7. **Test and iterate:** Review your chart to ensure it accurately represents the data and effectively communicates your message. Share it with colleagues or stakeholders for feedback. Iterate and make adjustments as necessary to improve clarity and visual impact.

8. **Consider interactivity**: If appropriate, consider adding interactivity to your chart or graph. Interactive elements allow users to explore the data further, change variables or filters, and gain deeper insights. This can be especially useful when presenting data in dashboards or online platforms.

Remember that creating charts and graphs requires a balance between aesthetics and data accuracy. Ensure that your visualization accurately represents the underlying data and that it is visually appealing and easy to understand. Clever design choices and thoughtful presentation can greatly enhance the impact of your chart or graph.

Customizing Chart Elements

Customizing chart elements is an essential step in creating effective and visually appealing charts and graphs.
Here are some key elements you can customize to enhance your visualization:

1. **Titles and labels**: Provide clear and descriptive titles for your chart and axes. Make sure they accurately reflect the data being presented and the message you want to convey. Use informative labels for each axis to indicate the data variables and units of measurement.

2. **Axis scales and ranges:** Adjust the scaling and ranges of your chart axes to ensure the data is properly represented. You can choose linear or logarithmic scales, set minimum and maximum values, and specify intervals or tick marks for better readability.

3. **Colors and visual styles:** Select appropriate colors and visual styles that complement your data and add visual interest. Use color palettes that are easy on the eyes and provide sufficient contrast for different data categories or groups. Consider using gradients or shading to show variations or trends in the data.

4. **Legends and annotations:** Include a legend to help users understand the meaning of different colors, symbols, or patterns used in your chart. Use annotations such as data point labels, callouts, or explanatory text boxes to provide additional context or highlight important observations.

5. **Data markers and lines**: Customize the shape, size, and style of data markers (e.g., points, bars) and lines (e.g., line thickness, style) to distinguish different data series or categories. This helps make your chart more visually appealing and easily readable.

6. **Gridlines and background**: Add gridlines to guide the reader's eye and provide reference points. Determine whether horizontal or vertical gridlines are necessary and adjust their opacity or style as needed. Choose an appropriate background color or pattern that complements the overall design and doesn't distract from the data.

7. **Chart layout and formatting:** Consider the overall layout and formatting of your chart. Align chart elements, such as titles, axes, and legends, in a visually pleasing manner. Adjust the size and proportions of the chart to fit the space available and ensure readability. Pay attention to font styles, sizes, and colors to maintain consistency and enhance clarity.

8. **Animation and interactivity**: If you are creating an interactive or dynamic chart, explore options to animate or add interactive features. This can include transitions between data states, tooltips for data points, or hover effects that provide additional information when the user interacts with the chart.

When customizing chart elements, it's important to strike a balance between visual appeal and data accuracy. Avoid embellishing or distorting the data for the sake of aesthetics. Instead, focus on highlighting the key insights and trends while providing a clear and understandable representation of the data.

Working with Chart Types and Layouts

Working with different chart types and layouts can greatly impact the effectiveness and clarity of your visualizations.

Here are some tips for working with chart types and layouts:

1. **Understand the data**: Before choosing a chart type, it's important to understand the nature of your data and the insights you want to communicate. Consider the variables being measured, the level of granularity, and the relationships between different data points.

2. **Choose the right chart type**: There are various chart types available, such as line charts, bar charts, pie charts, scatter plots, and more. Each chart type has its own strengths and suitability for different types of data. For example, use a line chart to show trends over time, a bar chart for comparisons between different categories, or a scatter plot for showing relationships between variables.

3. **Simplify the visualization**: Avoid cluttering your chart with excessive data points or unnecessary details. Maintain simplicity by focusing on the most important data points and removing any distractions or unnecessary embellishments. Decluttering your chart will make it easier for viewers to interpret and understand the information being presented.

4. **Consider the audience**: Tailor the chart type and layout to the target audience. Choose a chart type that is familiar to the audience and aligns with their preferences and prior knowledge. For example, if your audience is primarily executives or stakeholders, a simple and visually appealing chart with clear callouts is likely to be more effective than a complex one.

5. **Experiment with different** layouts: Choose a layout that best supports the narrative and message you want to convey. Consider the placement and arrangement of chart elements, such as axes, legends, and titles. For example, you can position the axis labels horizontally or vertically, place the legend inside or outside the chart area, or include multiple charts side by side for comparisons.

6. **Use multiple chart types together**: Sometimes, combining multiple chart types can provide a more comprehensive view of the data. For example, you can use a combination of line and bar charts to show both trends and comparisons. This can help viewers understand different aspects of the data and draw meaningful insights.

7. **Test and iterate**: It's essential to test your chart types and layouts with a sample audience to ensure they are effectively conveying your intended message. Gather feedback and make iterative adjustments based on the audience's understanding and preferences.

Remember, the goal of using different chart types and layouts is to present data in a clear and visually appealing way that effectively communicates insights and trends. Always prioritize accuracy and readability over aesthetics, and choose chart types and layouts that best suit the data and the needs of your audience.

Adding Chart Titles and Labels

Adding chart titles and labels is an important step in creating clear and understandable visualizations.

Here are some tips for effectively adding chart titles and labels:

1. **Include a descriptive chart title:** Start by giving your chart a clear and concise title that accurately reflects the main message or purpose of the visualization. The title should provide context and help viewers understand what they are looking at. For example, if you are showing sales data over time, a suitable title could be "Quarterly Sales Performance (2018-2020)."

2. **Label your axes:** Axes labels are crucial for understanding the variables being measured in your chart. Make sure to label each axis with a clear and concise description that indicates the units of measurement. For instance, if you have a bar chart comparing product sales by region, label the x-axis as "Region" and the y-axis as "Sales (in thousands)."

3. **Use appropriate data labels**: Data labels can provide additional information about specific data points within your chart. Depending on the chart type and purpose, you might choose to include labels such as actual values, percentages, or annotations. Use data labels sparingly and ensure they are not overwhelming or cluttering the chart.

4. **Add a legend**: If your chart includes multiple data series or categories, including a legend can help clarify what each color or symbol represents. Place the legend outside the chart area if possible, and use clear and concise labels to ensure viewers can easily associate each color or symbol with the corresponding data series.

5. **Consider positioning and formatting**: Pay attention to the positioning and formatting of your chart titles and labels. Ensure they are easily readable and not obscured by other elements. Adjust the font size, color, and style to make them stand out but maintain consistency with the overall design of your visualization.

6. **Align titles and labels with the chart**: Make sure your chart titles and labels are visually aligned with the relevant chart elements. For example, align the chart title at the top of the chart and the axis labels along the respective axes. This alignment helps viewers quickly connect the title and labels with the corresponding data.

7. **Keep titles and labels simple and** clear: Avoid using jargon or overly technical terms in your chart titles and labels. Use language that is easily understood by your target audience. Keep the titles and labels concise, ensuring they communicate the necessary information without unnecessary detail.

By adding clear and descriptive titles and labels, you can enhance the clarity and understanding of your visualizations. These elements play a crucial role in guiding viewers through the data and conveying the intended message effectively.

Collaboration and Sharing

Collaboration and sharing are essential components of effective data visualization. Here are some tips on how to collaborate and share visualizations with others:

1. **Choose the right tools**: Use tools that facilitate collaboration and sharing of visualizations. There are various options available, ranging from cloud-based platforms to desktop software. Consider features such as real-time collaboration, sharing permissions, and the ability to export or embed visualizations in different formats.

2. **Share visualizations securely:** If you are working with sensitive or confidential data, ensure that the sharing and collaboration platform you choose has appropriate security measures in place. This may include data encryption, secure user authentication, access controls, and audit trails.

3. **Define collaboration roles and responsibilities**: Clearly define roles and responsibilities for each person involved in the collaboration process. Determine who will be responsible for creating the visualizations, analyzing the data, reviewing and providing feedback, and finalizing the visualizations for sharing.

4. **Establish communication channels**: Use effective communication channels to facilitate collaboration and feedback. This may include regular meetings, video conferences, email, or collaboration tools with built-in messaging features. Encourage open communication and the sharing of ideas and insights.

5. **Provide context and documentation**: When sharing visualizations, provide context and documentation to help users understand the data, the analysis process, and any specific insights or findings. This could include a brief summary, a data dictionary, or a methodology document.

6. **Incorporate feedback**: Encourage feedback from collaborators and stakeholders to improve the visualizations. Take into account different perspectives and suggestions to enhance the clarity, accuracy, and usefulness of the visualizations. Iteratively refine the visualizations based on the feedback received.

7. **Consider version control**: If multiple team members are working simultaneously on the visualizations, implement version control mechanisms to track changes and avoid conflicting modifications. This ensures that everyone is working on the latest version and maintains a history of revisions.

8. **Make sharing interactive**: Consider sharing interactive visualizations that allow users to explore the data and customize their views. Interactive features such as filtering, sorting, and drill-down capabilities can enhance the user experience and facilitate deeper understanding.

9. **Share across different platforms and mediums**: Share your visualizations across relevant platforms and mediums to reach a wider audience. This may include sharing dashboards on web platforms, embedding visualizations in presentations or reports, or sharing static images or PDFs through email or social media.

10. **Obtain feedback and** iterate: Once you have shared your visualizations, actively seek feedback from the audience or users. Analyze their responses and iterate on the visualizations as necessary to improve their effectiveness and address any concerns or suggestions.

Effective collaboration and sharing of visualizations can lead to better insights, decision-making, and understanding among team members and stakeholders. By implementing these tips, you can ensure that your visualizations are well-received and effectively communicated to the intended audience.

Protecting worksheets and workbooks

Protecting worksheets and workbooks is crucial to safeguard the integrity and security of your data.

Here are some important steps to follow when protecting your worksheets and workbooks:

- ☐ **Password protect your worksheets**: Excel and other spreadsheet software allow you to set passwords to protect specific worksheets. By setting a password, you can control who can make changes to the data or formatting in that particular worksheet. It is important to choose a strong password that is not easily guessable, and to keep a record of the password in a secure location.
- ☐ **Protect workbook structure**: In addition to protecting specific worksheets, you can also protect the entire workbook structure. This prevents anyone from inserting, deleting, or renaming worksheets without the necessary password. Workbook structure protection is particularly useful when you want to maintain the integrity of the workbook's organization.
- ☐ **Protect workbook windows**: You can protect workbook windows to prevent modifications to the window size, position, or view settings. This prevents users from accidentally or intentionally changing the layout of the workbook. Password protect the workbook windows to ensure only authorized individuals can make changes.
- ☐ **Protect cells or ranges**: To restrict modifications to specific cells or ranges within a worksheet, you can protect those cells. This allows you to maintain the integrity of critical data while still allowing users to input data into other cells. For example, you can protect formulas or important headings while leaving the rest of the worksheet editable.

☐ **Limit editing to specific users:** If you are collaborating with multiple people on a workbook, you can restrict editing access to specific users. This ensures that only authorized individuals can modify the workbook, while others may have read-only access. This feature is particularly useful when you want to control who can make changes to the workbook in a collaborative environment.

☐ **Hide formulas**: To protect sensitive formulas or calculations, you can hide them from view. This prevents accidental modification or unauthorized access to critical formulas. However, it is important to note that hiding formulas does not provide 100% security, as more experienced users may still be able to uncover hidden formulas.

☐ **Protect workbook from sharing or distributing**: If you want to prevent the workbook from being shared or distributed without your permission, you can consider using digital rights management (DRM) tools. DRM tools secure your workbook by employing encryption and access controls, and they can help protect your workbook from unauthorized sharing or distribution.

☐ **Regularly backup your workbooks**: In case of accidental data loss, it is essential to regularly backup your workbooks. Create backups of your protected workbooks and save them in a secure location. This ensures that even if your protected workbooks become corrupt or compromised, you can restore a previous version.

Remember, while these protection measures can help safeguard your worksheets and workbooks, they are not foolproof. It is essential to regularly review and update your security practices, including using antivirus software, keeping your software up to date, and educating yourself and others about potential security risks.

Sharing workbooks with others

Sharing workbooks with others is a common practice, especially in a collaborative work environment. It allows multiple individuals to access and work on the same workbook simultaneously.

Here are some important tips to consider when sharing workbooks with others:

- **Choose the right collaboration platform**: There are various collaboration platforms available that allow multiple users to work on the same workbook. Some popular options include cloud storage services like Google Drive, Microsoft OneDrive, or collaboration features in spreadsheet software like Google Sheets or Microsoft Excel.
- **Set permissions and access levels**: Before sharing a workbook, determine the level of access you want to grant to other users. Some collaboration platforms allow you to set permissions, such as read-only access, editing access, or commenting access. It is important to carefully consider who needs what level of access to the workbook.
- **Communicate clearly with collaborators**: When sharing a workbook with others, clearly communicate your expectations and guidelines for working on the workbook. If there are specific formatting rules, data entry guidelines, or areas that should not be modified, make sure to communicate those to your collaborators.
- **Version control**: When multiple users are working on the same workbook, it is important to establish a version control system. This ensures that everyone is working on the most up-to-date version of the workbook. Consider using features like track changes or revision history available in collaboration platforms to keep track of changes made by different users.
- **Resolve conflicts and discrepancies**: In a collaborative environment, conflicts and discrepancies may arise when multiple users are making changes to the workbook simultaneously. If conflicts occur (e.g., when two users modify the same cell), communication and collaboration become crucial to resolve the conflicts and ensure data integrity.

- **Secure data and protect sensitive information**: When sharing workbooks with others, it is important to consider the security of your data. Avoid sharing sensitive information, such as passwords or personal data, in shared workbooks unless absolutely necessary. If sensitive information must be shared, ensure that appropriate security measures, such as encryption, are in place.
- **Regularly back up the shared workbook**: As multiple users are working on the shared workbook, it is important to regularly back up the file to prevent data loss. Create backup copies of the workbook and keep them in a secure location. This enables you to restore a previous version in case of accidental data loss or corruption.
- **Review and finalize the workbook**: Once all collaborators have finished their contributions, it is important to thoroughly review and finalize the workbook. Check for any errors, inconsistencies, or formatting issues, and ensure that the workbook is ready for its intended purpose before sharing it further or using it for important tasks.

By following these tips, you can effectively share workbooks with others, collaborate efficiently, and maintain the integrity and security of your data.

Tracking changes and comments

Tracking changes and comments is an important aspect of sharing workbooks with others, especially in a collaborative environment. It allows you to keep track of modifications made by different users and facilitates effective communication and feedback.

Here are some tips for effectively tracking changes and adding comments in shared workbooks:

1. **Enable track changes**: Before sharing the workbook, enable the track changes feature available in your spreadsheet software. This feature will keep a record of all the modifications made to the workbook, including changes made to cells, formatting, and formulas.
2. **Set tracking options:** Depending on the collaboration platform or spreadsheet software you are using, you may have various tracking options available. Set the tracking options based on your preferences and needs. For example, you can choose whether to track changes made by everyone or only specific users, and whether to track changes to formatting or only to the actual data.
3. **Review changes**: Regularly review the tracked changes to stay updated on modifications made by other users. This helps you stay informed about the progress and ensures that you are working on the most up-to-date version of the workbook.
4. **Resolve conflicts**: When multiple users make changes to the same cells simultaneously or change conflicting data, conflicts may occur. It is important to address these conflicts promptly and collaborate with other users to resolve them. Communication is key in resolving conflicts and ensuring data integrity.
5. **Use comments and annotations:** Adding comments and annotations to specific cells or sections of the workbook can provide additional context or instructions for other users. Comments allow users to ask questions, provide explanations, or give feedback on specific parts of the workbook. They can enhance collaboration and facilitate effective communication.

6. **Respond to comments**: When other users add comments to the workbook, make sure to respond and address their queries or feedback in a timely manner. This helps create an interactive and constructive collaboration environment.

7. **Finalize comments and changes**: After all collaborators have reviewed and made their modifications, it is important to finalize the comments and changes. Ensure that all feedback and comments have been addressed, and consider accepting or rejecting tracked changes based on the relevance and accuracy.

8. **Keep a clean, readable version:** Once all changes and comments have been reviewed and accepted, it is a good practice to save a clean, finalized version of the workbook. This version should have all the necessary modifications incorporated and unnecessary comments removed to ensure a readable and professional workbook.

By effectively tracking changes and using comments, you can enhance communication, collaboration, and data integrity in shared workbooks. It helps users stay informed, provide feedback, and establish a transparent and efficient workflow.

Collaborating on shared workbooks

Collaborating on shared workbooks is a valuable way to work on projects or tasks with multiple team members. Whether you are working on a budget spreadsheet, a project timeline, or any other type of shared workbook, collaborating allows everyone to contribute their expertise and work together toward a common goal.

Here are some tips for collaborating effectively on shared workbooks:

1. **Choose the right collaboration platform**: There are various collaboration platforms available, such as Google Sheets, Microsoft Excel Online, or cloud-based project management tools. Choose a platform that suits your team's needs and preferences. Consider factors like real-time editing, version control, and ease of use.

2. **Set up permissions and sharing settings**: Be mindful of the permissions and sharing settings you set for the shared workbook. Determine who can view, edit, or comment on the workbook. This helps maintain security and privacy while ensuring that only authorized individuals can make changes.

3. **Communicate and establish clear roles**: Effective communication is crucial when collaborating on a shared workbook. Establish clear roles and responsibilities for team members to avoid duplication of efforts and confusion. Regularly communicate about progress, deadlines, and any obstacles encountered during the collaboration process.

4. Break down tasks and assign responsibilities: Divide the workbook into specific sections or tasks that can be assigned to different team members. Clearly define these tasks and assign them to individuals based on their skills and expertise. This helps distribute the workload evenly and allows everyone to take ownership of their assigned tasks.

5. **Use real-time collaboration features:** If your collaboration platform supports real-time editing, take advantage of this feature. It allows multiple team members to work on the workbook simultaneously, eliminating the need for constant file sharing and version control. Real-time collaboration promotes efficiency and enables instant feedback and discussions.

6. **Share updates and progress regularly:** Keep the team updated on the progress of the shared workbook. Provide frequent updates on completed tasks, milestones, or any changes made. This keeps everyone informed and helps maintain a transparent and streamlined workflow.

7. **Review and validate changes:** Encourage team members to thoroughly review their changes before finalizing them. Ensure that the modifications made align with the project's objectives and adhere to any established guidelines. This helps maintain the accuracy and integrity of the shared workbook.

8. Schedule regular meetings or check-ins: In addition to online collaboration, schedule regular meetings or check-ins to discuss progress, address any issues, or provide clarifications. These meetings facilitate open communication, allow for deeper discussions, and help keep the team focused and aligned.

9. **Document feedback and decisions**: When collaborating on a shared workbook, it is important to document any feedback, decisions, or changes made. This documentation serves as a reference tool, helping team members track the evolution of the project and understand the reasoning behind certain choices.

10. **Celebrate achievements and acknowledge contributions**: Finally, celebrate achievements and acknowledge the contributions of team members. Recognize their efforts and express gratitude for their collaboration. This helps foster a positive team dynamic and motivates individuals to continue working together effectively.

Collaborating on shared workbooks offers numerous benefits, including increased productivity, improved accuracy, and stronger teamwork. By following these tips, you can create an effective and seamless collaboration environment, leading to successful outcomes for your projects.

Advanced Excel Features

Advanced Excel features refer to the more complex and powerful functionalities that Excel offers beyond basic calculations and data organization. These features can greatly enhance productivity, data analysis, and visualization capabilities.

Here are some advanced Excel features that can take your spreadsheet skills to the next level:

1. **PivotTables**: PivotTables allow you to summarize, analyze, and present large amounts of data in a concise and meaningful way. This feature enables you to group, filter, and rearrange data dynamically, providing insights and allowing you to see trends and patterns.

2. **Macros**: Macros are recorded sets of actions that automate repetitive tasks in Excel. By recording a series of steps, such as formatting, data sorting, or calculations, you can create a macro that can be executed with a single click, saving time and effort.

3. **Data Validation**: Data Validation helps ensure data integrity by limiting the values that users can enter into a cell. You can set rules, such as allowing only certain types of data (e.g., dates or numbers within a specific range) or creating drop-down lists to select from predefined options.

4. **Conditional Formatting**: Conditional Formatting allows you to dynamically format cells based on specific criteria. This feature helps highlight important data, identify trends, and create visual alerts. You can format cells based on values, formulas, or even with data bars, color scales, or icon sets.

5. **Goal Seek and Solver**: Goal Seek and Solver are tools for finding solutions to problems involving variables. Goal Seek lets you determine the value of a cell needed to achieve a desired outcome. Solver is more complex and can

solve optimization problems by adjusting multiple variables based on defined constraints.

6. **Power Query**: Power Query is a powerful data connection and transformation tool in Excel. It allows you to import, transform, and shape data from various sources and combine them into a single data model. Power Query simplifies data cleaning, merging, and analysis.

7. **Advanced Formulas**: Excel offers a wide range of advanced formulas for complex calculations. Functions like VLOOKUP, INDEX-MATCH, SUMIFS, and IFERROR are commonly used to perform more sophisticated data analysis and manipulations.

8. **Data Analysis ToolPak**: The Data Analysis ToolPak is an Excel add-in that provides various statistical and analytical tools. It includes features like regression analysis, random number generation, sampling, and moving averages. Enabling the ToolPak expands your data analysis capabilities.

9. **Charts and Graphs**: Excel offers a wide variety of chart types, including column, line, pie, and scatter plots. You can customize charts with different colors, styles, and elements. Advanced chart features include adding trendlines, chart templates, and dynamic updating based on changing data.

10. **Visual Basic for Applications (VBA):** VBA is a programming language that allows you to write custom macros and automate repetitive tasks in Excel. With VBA, you can create interactive user interfaces, perform complex calculations, and integrate Excel with other applications.

By mastering these advanced Excel features, you can become more efficient in data manipulation, analysis, and presentation. These features provide greater flexibility and functionality, enabling you to work with larger datasets, automate tasks, and draw more meaningful insights from your data.

Using Macros for Automation

Using macros for automation in Excel can greatly enhance your productivity and efficiency. Macros allow you to record a series of actions and then replay them with a single click, automating repetitive tasks and saving you time and effort.

Here are some key points to consider when using macros for automation:

1. **Recording a Macro**: To record a macro, go to the "Developer" tab (if it's not visible, enable it in Excel settings) and click on the "Record Macro" button. Give your macro a name, choose where to store it, and optionally assign it a shortcut key. Once you start recording, Excel will track all your actions until you stop recording.

2. **Automating Repetitive Tasks**: Macros are perfect for automating repetitive tasks such as formatting data, applying formulas, or performing calculations. For example, if you often need to apply the same formatting to a range of cells, you can record a macro that does it for you, and then replay it whenever you need.

3. **Customizing and Editing Macros**: After recording a macro, you can customize and edit it using the Visual Basic for Applications (VBA) editor. This enables you to make adjustments, add additional functionality, or write your own code. The VBA editor provides a wide range of tools and functions to enhance the capabilities of your macros.

4. **Adding User Interaction**: Macros can also include user input and interaction. By creating custom dialog boxes or input forms, you can collect information from users and use it to perform specific actions. For example, you can create a macro that prompts the user to enter values and then performs calculations based on those inputs.

5. **Running Macros**: After recording and editing a macro, you can run it by clicking on the assigned shortcut key or selecting it from the Macro list in the "Developer" tab. Depending on your needs, you can run macros on a selected range, a specific worksheet, or the entire workbook.

6. **Error Handling**: When writing or recording macros, it's important to include error handling to handle unexpected situations or user errors. By using error-handling routines and error-checking functions, you can ensure that your macros run smoothly and provide the desired results.

7. **Sharing and Distributing Macros**: Excel macros can be shared and distributed among colleagues or partners. You can save your macros in a separate Excel file or share them as an add-in (.xlam). Add-ins can be loaded in Excel, allowing users to access the macros without having to create them from scratch.

8. **Security Considerations**: It's crucial to be cautious when running macros, as they can potentially execute malicious code. Excel provides security options that allow you to control macro execution, such as enabling or disabling macros, or limiting macros to digitally signed sources. Always ensure that macros come from trusted sources and be mindful of macro security settings to protect yourself and your data.

Using macros for automation in Excel can significantly improve your workflow and productivity. By automating repetitive tasks, you can save time, reduce errors, and focus on more complex analysis and decision-making. Whether you're formatting data, performing calculations, or creating custom functionality, macros are a powerful tool to streamline your Excel workflow.

Importing and Exporting Data

Importing and exporting data is an essential task in Excel that allows you to transfer information between different applications or files. Whether you need to bring data into Excel from an external source or export Excel data to another format, understanding the options and techniques for importing and exporting can greatly enhance your data management capabilities.

Here are some key points to consider when working with importing and exporting data in Excel:

Importing Data:
a. Import from File: Excel supports importing data from various file formats, including CSV, TXT, XML, JSON, Access databases, and more. You can use the "Get External Data" option in the "Data" tab to connect to an external data source and import data into Excel.

b. Import from Database: Excel also allows you to directly connect to and import data from databases such as SQL Server, Oracle, MySQL, etc. This enables you to retrieve data from specific tables or queries and bring it into Excel for further analysis or manipulation.

c. Importing Web Data: If you need to import data from a website or web page, you can use the "From Web" option in the "Data" tab. Excel will prompt you to specify the webpage URL and then automatically retrieve and import the data.

d. Importing Text Files: When importing data from a text file, you can define the delimiters used to separate columns and specify the data type for each column.

Excel provides a Text Import Wizard to guide you through the import process and ensure the data is formatted correctly.

Exporting Data:

a. **Export to File:** Excel allows you to export data to various file formats, such as CSV, TXT, PDF, XML, HTML, and more. To export data, select the range of cells you want to export and choose the appropriate export option from the "File" or "Save As" menu. This creates a new file with the exported data in the specified format.

b. **Export to Database**: In addition to importing data from databases, Excel enables you to export data to databases as well. By establishing a connection to the database and mapping the Excel data to specific tables or queries, you can transfer your Excel data back into the database for further use or analysis.

c. **Exporting Charts and Reports**: Excel allows you to save charts, graphs, and reports as image files or PDFs. By selecting the desired chart or report and using the "Save As" or "Export" options, you can create visual representations of your data for sharing or presentation purposes.

Data Connection and Refresh:

When importing data from external sources, Excel provides options to establish a data connection and refresh the imported data automatically. This is particularly useful when working with dynamic data that frequently changes. By setting up data connections and defining refresh intervals, you can ensure that your data stays up to date without the need for manual re-importing.

Mapping and Transforming Data:

Excel allows you to map and transform imported data to match the structure and formatting required in your workbook. The "Power Query" feature in Excel provides a powerful set of tools for cleaning, transforming, and shaping data imported from various sources. You can use Power Query to remove duplicates, filter data, split columns, merge data, or perform calculations before importing the data into your Excel workbook.

External Data Queries:

Excel provides the ability to create external data queries, also known as connections, which allow you to retrieve and import data from external sources directly into your workbook. By creating a connection to a data source and building a query, you can customize the data import process and regularly update the imported data from within Excel.

Importing and exporting data in Excel is a fundamental skill that can greatly improve your data management and analysis capabilities. Whether you need to import data for analysis or distribute data to other systems or applications, Excel provides a variety of tools and options to facilitate the import and export process. By understanding these techniques, you can efficiently transfer data and integrate it into your Excel workflows.

Linking data between worksheets and workbooks

Linking data between worksheets and workbooks in Excel allows you to create connections and references between different sheets or files, enabling you to update and manipulate data in one location while reflecting changes in other locations. This capability is especially useful when you need to consolidate data from multiple sources or analyze data across different worksheets or workbooks.

Here are some important points to consider when linking data between worksheets and workbooks:

Linking within a Workbook:

a. **Cell References**: The simplest and most common way to link data between worksheets in the same workbook is by using cell references. By selecting a cell in one worksheet and entering a formula that references a specific cell in another worksheet, you can retrieve or display data dynamically. For example, to link data from cell A1 in Sheet1 to cell B1 in Sheet2, you can enter "=Sheet1!A1" in cell B1 of Sheet2.

b. **Named Ranges**: Named ranges allow you to assign a name to a specific range of cells in a worksheet. By creating named ranges, you can simplify the process of linking data between worksheets. Instead of using cell references, you can use the named range in formulas to reference the desired data. This can make your formulas easier to understand and maintain.

Linking between Workbooks:

a. **External References**: When linking data between different workbooks, you can use external references to establish connections. External references allow you to reference cells or ranges in another workbook by specifying the source workbook and the cell or range address. For example, to link to a cell in another workbook, you can enter "= [Workbook Name]Sheet1!A1" in a cell of the current workbook. If the source workbook is open, Excel will maintain a live link that updates automatically when changes are made in the source workbook.

b. **Clipboard Options**: If you need to copy data from one workbook to another without establishing a connection, you can use the clipboard options in Excel. By copying the desired data from the source workbook and pasting it into the destination workbook as a link, you can create a one-time connection that pulls data from the source workbook into the destination workbook. However, this link will not update automatically if changes are made in the source workbook.

Updating Linked Data:

a. **Automatic Calculation**: Excel provides options for controlling the calculation and updating of linked data. By default, Excel automatically recalculates formulas and updates linked data whenever changes are made in a source cell. However, you can modify the calculation settings in the "Formulas" tab and choose manual calculation if you prefer to update linked data manually.

b. **Refreshing External Links**: When linking data between workbooks, the source workbook may contain external links to other workbooks or files. Excel provides the option to manually or automatically refresh these external links to update the linked data. You can find the "Edit Links" option in the "Data" tab, which allows you to manage and update external links.

Linking data between worksheets and workbooks in Excel provides a powerful way to consolidate and analyze data from various sources. Whether you need to create dynamic reports, track changes in data, or perform complex calculations, understanding how to link data between worksheets and workbooks can greatly enhance your data management and analysis capabilities in Excel.

Creating and Formatting Pivot Charts

Creating and formatting pivot charts in Excel allows you to visually summarize and analyze data from a pivot table. A pivot chart is a graphical representation of data generated from a pivot table, enabling you to gain insights and present data in a more intuitive and interactive way.

Here's a step-by-step guide on how to create and format pivot charts:

Create a Pivot Table:

1. Select the data range you want to analyze.

2. Go to the "Insert" tab and click on "PivotTable" (in newer versions of Excel, you may find it under the "Tables" group).

3. Choose the source data and select the location for the pivot table (e.g., a new worksheet or an existing worksheet).

4. Click "OK" to create the pivot table.

Create the Pivot Chart:

1. Select any cell within the pivot table.

2. In the "PivotTable Analyze" or "Analyze" tab (depending on your Excel version), click on "PivotChart" (usually located in the "Tools" group).

3. Choose the desired chart type from the available options (e.g., bar chart, line chart, pie chart, etc.).

4. Select the chart location (e.g., new worksheet or existing worksheet).

5. Click "OK" to create the pivot chart.

Format the Pivot Chart:

1. Click on the pivot chart to activate the "Chart Tools" tab.

2. In the "Design" tab, you can choose from various chart styles and color schemes to customize the appearance of the pivot chart.

3. Use the "Chart Layouts" and "Chart Elements" options to add or remove chart elements such as titles, legends, axis labels, data labels, and gridlines.

4. Select a specific chart element (e.g., data series, axes, or plot area) and right-click to access additional formatting options.

5. Change the chart type if needed by clicking on the "Change Chart Type" button in the "Design" tab and selecting a new chart type.

6. Use the "Chart Filters" option in the "Analyze" or "PivotTable Analyze" tab to filter or hide specific data series or categories in the pivot chart.

7. Adjust the size and position of the chart on the worksheet as desired.

Update the Pivot Chart:

1. Any changes made to the pivot table (such as adding or removing fields, changing field settings, or refreshing data) will automatically update the linked pivot chart.

2. To manually refresh the pivot chart, right-click on the chart and choose "Refresh" or go to the "Analyze" or "PivotTable Analyze" tab and click on "Refresh".

By creating and formatting pivot charts in Excel, you can effectively visualize and analyze your data, making it easier to identify trends, patterns, and relationships. Experiment with different chart types and formatting options to suit your specific requirements and enhance the overall presentation and analysis of your data.

Conclusion on Microsoft Excel

In conclusion,By mastering the basics of Excel, such as navigating the interface, creating and formatting worksheets, applying formulas and functions, working with data formats, and organizing and analyzing data through filters and sorting, we have gained the necessary skills to efficiently handle and manipulate data.

Furthermore, the training has covered advanced topics, including creating and formatting charts and pivot tables, implementing conditional formatting, utilizing data validation, and automating tasks with macros. These advanced functionalities allow for more sophisticated data analysis and reporting, ultimately improving productivity and decision-making processes.

Overall, the training in Microsoft Excel has enhanced our ability to organize, analyze, and visualize data to extract meaningful insights and facilitate data-driven decision-making. Excel's versatility and wide range of features make it an indispensable tool in various industries, such as finance, marketing, operations, and project management.

As we continue to practice and explore the features of Excel, we will become more proficient in using this software, allowing us to save time, reduce errors, and effectively manage and analyze data. The skills acquired in this training will undoubtedly contribute to our professional growth and increase our value in the workplace.

Introduction to Microsoft PowerPoint

Microsoft PowerPoint is a powerful presentation software that allows users to create dynamic and visually appealing slideshows. It is widely used in various professional settings, such as business, education, and training, to effectively communicate ideas and information to an audience.

PowerPoint offers a range of features and tools that enable users to create engaging and professional presentations. With its user-friendly interface, even beginners can quickly navigate the software and start creating slides.

The software offers different views and layouts, allowing users to easily organize and structure their presentation. Users can add and edit text, format font styles, sizes, colors, and effects, and insert images, shapes, charts, tables, and multimedia elements to enhance the visual appeal of their slides.

One of the key features of PowerPoint is the Slide Master, which allows users to create consistent formatting and design throughout the presentation. By modifying the Slide Master layouts and designs, users can achieve a unified look and feel across all slides.

PowerPoint also offers various tools for enhancing slide content, such as animations, transitions, and multimedia integration. These features can be used to add visual interest and engage the audience during the presentation.

In addition to creating slideshows, PowerPoint also offers capabilities for presenting and sharing presentations. Users can customize slide show options, such as slide timings and transitions, rehearse and deliver presentations effectively, and customize slide show navigation and interaction. PowerPoint also provides options for printing and distributing presentations and collaborating with others in real-time using PowerPoint Online.

Mastering Microsoft PowerPoint is essential in today's digital age, where presentations play a significant role in conveying information and ideas. Whether it's for sales pitches, educational lectures, or business reports, PowerPoint provides a platform for creating impactful and professional presentations.

In this training course, you will gain a comprehensive understanding of PowerPoint's features and learn how to create engaging and visually appealing presentations. They will be equipped with the skills to effectively communicate ideas and information, enhance the impact and engagement of their slides, and deliver presentations with confidence.

Overview of PowerPoint Interface and Features

The PowerPoint interface is designed to be user-friendly and intuitive, allowing users to navigate and use the software easily. The interface consists of various elements and features that enable users to create, edit, and present their slideshows effectively.

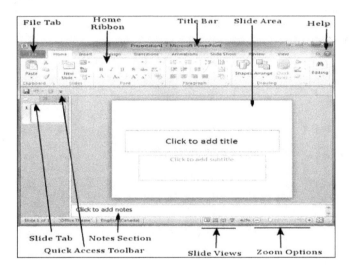

PowerPoint Interface

1. **Ribbon**: The Ribbon is the main toolbar at the top of the PowerPoint window. It contains different tabs, such as Home, Insert, Design, Transitions, Animations, and more. Each tab contains groups of related tools and commands that users can access to format and customize their slides.

2. **Slides pane**: The Slides pane is located on the left side of the PowerPoint window. It provides an overview of the slides in the presentation, allowing users to easily navigate and rearrange them. Users can add, delete, and duplicate slides from this pane.

3. **Slide layout**: Each slide in PowerPoint is based on a specific layout, which determines the arrangement of placeholders for text, images, charts, and other content. Users can choose different slide layouts from the Slide Layout options in the Home tab.

4. **Placeholder**: A placeholder is a pre-formatted area on a slide where users can insert and modify text, images, charts, and other types of content. PowerPoint provides various types of placeholders, such as Title, Content, Picture, and SmartArt, to accommodate different types of slide content.

5. **Slide Master**: The Slide Master is a feature that allows users to define the overall formatting and design of their presentation. By modifying the Slide Master, users can apply consistent styles, fonts, colors, and backgrounds to all slides in the presentation.

6. **Animation and Transition effects**: PowerPoint offers a wide range of animation and transition effects to enhance the visual appeal and engagement of slides. Users can apply animations to individual elements within a slide and transitions between slides to create a dynamic and professional presentation.

7. **Media integration**: PowerPoint allows users to insert various types of media, such as images, videos, audio clips, and online content, into their slides. Users can resize, crop, and format these media elements to suit their presentation needs.

8. **Presenter View**: When delivering a presentation, PowerPoint offers Presenter View, which provides a dual-screen setup. The presenter's screen displays the current slide, speaker notes, and a timer, while the audience sees only the slide on the main screen. This feature helps presenters to deliver presentations smoothly and confidently.

9. **Collaboration and sharing**: PowerPoint provides options for collaborating with others in real-time using PowerPoint Online. Multiple users can work on a presentation simultaneously, making it easy to collaborate and share ideas. Users can also save presentations in various formats, such as PDF or PowerPoint Show, and distribute them to others.

Overall, Microsoft PowerPoint offers a comprehensive set of features and tools that allow users to create professional and engaging presentations. By utilizing the interface and features effectively, users can effectively communicate their ideas and information and make a lasting impact on their audience.

Understanding the different views and layouts in PowerPoint

PowerPoint offers various views and layouts to help users create and edit their presentations effectively. These views and layouts provide different perspectives on the slide content and allow users to customize the design and organization of their slides. Understanding these options can greatly enhance the productivity and visual appeal of your PowerPoint presentations.

Let's take a closer look at the different views and layouts in PowerPoint.

1. **Normal View**: The Normal view is the default view in PowerPoint, providing a workspace where users can create and edit slides. In this view, users can see the slide thumbnails on the left pane, the slide itself in the middle, and the Notes pane at the bottom for adding speaker notes. The Normal view allows users to work on individual slides and make adjustments to their content and layout.

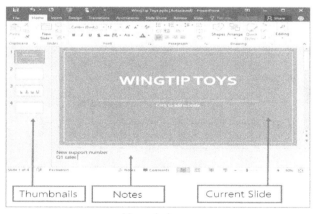

Normal view

2. **Slide Sorter View**: The Slide Sorter view displays all slides in a presentation as thumbnails in a grid. This view allows users to easily reorder, delete, and duplicate slides. It is particularly useful when users need to rearrange their slides in a specific order or check the flow of their presentation.

slide sorter view

3. **Slide Show View**: The Slide Show view is used to deliver the presentation in full-screen mode. When in this view, the slide takes up the entire screen, providing a complete and immersive experience for the audience. Users can navigate through the slides using keyboard or mouse controls, and animations and transitions are activated during the presentation.

slide show view

4. **Reading View**: The Reading view provides a way to preview the presentation with larger slides and speaker notes. This view is useful for reviewing the content and layout of the slides before delivering the presentation. Users can also use the navigation controls to move through the slides or go to specific slides.

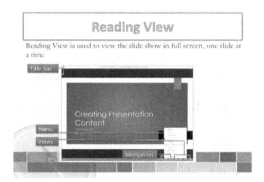

5. **Presenter View (available during slideshow):** Presenter View is a special view for presenters that offers a dual-screen setup. The presenter's screen displays the current slide, speaker notes, a timer, and other tools, while the audience sees only the slide on the main screen. This view allows presenters to have a complete overview of the presentation and control various aspects of the slideshow without distracting the audience.

Presenter view

6. **Slide Layouts**: PowerPoint provides a variety of pre-designed slide layouts that define the arrangement of placeholders for text, images, charts, and other content. Users can select a slide layout from the Layout options in the Home tab or Slide Master to choose the appropriate format for their slide content. Slide layouts help maintain consistency and make the presentation visually appealing.

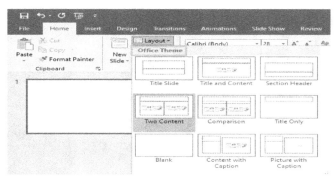

Slide layouts

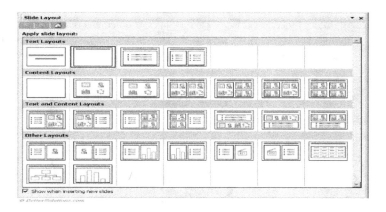

Slide layouts

7. **Slide Master**: The Slide Master is a powerful feature in PowerPoint that allows users to define the overall formatting and design for a presentation. By modifying the Slide Master, users can apply consistent styles, fonts, colors, and backgrounds to all slides in the presentation. Any changes made to the Slide Master are automatically reflected on all slides, ensuring a professional and cohesive look.

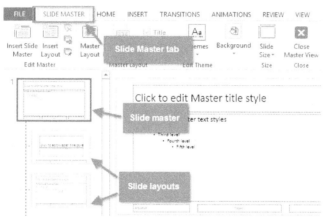

Slide Master

Understanding these different views and layouts in PowerPoint can significantly improve your productivity and enable you to create visually impressive presentations. By taking advantage of the various views and selecting appropriate slide layouts, you can effectively organize and customize your content to engage and captivate your audience.

Creating and Formatting Slides

Creating slides in Microsoft PowerPoint is a fundamental step in building a cohesive and visually appealing presentation. With PowerPoint's easy-to-use interface and powerful features, you can create professional-looking slides in no time.

Here are some tips on creating and formatting slides in PowerPoint:

1. **Adding a new slide**: To add a new slide, go to the Home tab and click on the "New Slide" button in the Slides group. You can choose from different slide layouts or use the default layout. Different layouts offer various placeholders for text, images, charts, and other content.

2. **Editing slide content**: To enter text on a slide, simply click on the text placeholder and start typing. You can modify the text font, size, color, alignment, and other formatting options using the options available in the Home tab's Font and Paragraph groups. You can also use the formatting options in the Mini Toolbar that appears when you select text.

3. **Adding images and media:** To insert an image or other media on a slide, go to the Insert tab and click on the "Pictures" or "Video" button. You can choose an image or video file from your computer or use the "Online Pictures" command to search for images on the web. You can resize and position the image or media on the slide, and even apply various formatting options like borders, filters, and effects.

4. **Using shapes and SmartArt**: PowerPoint provides a wide range of shapes and SmartArt graphics that can help highlight important points or illustrate concepts. To insert a shape or SmartArt, go to the Insert tab and click on the respective button. You can choose from different

shapes, modify their appearance, and even add animations and transitions to them.

5. **Applying slide transitions**: Slide transitions add visual effects when moving from one slide to another during a presentation. To apply a transition, go to the Transitions tab and choose a transition from the gallery. You can customize the transition duration, sound, and other settings. Be cautious, though, as excessive or inappropriate use of transitions can distract the audience and make the presentation less professional.

6. **Adding animations**: Animations can be applied to individual elements on a slide, such as text, images, and shapes, to control how they appear or move during the presentation. To add an animation, select the element and go to the Animations tab. Choose from the available animation options and customize the animation settings. Animations can help create visual interest and emphasize key points, but again, use them sparingly and appropriately.

7. **Using Slide Master for consistent formatting**: The Slide Master feature in PowerPoint allows you to define the overall formatting and design for your presentation. By modifying the Slide Master, you can apply consistent styles, fonts, colors, and backgrounds to all slides. This helps maintain a professional and cohesive look throughout the presentation. To access Slide Master, go to the View tab and click on the "Slide Master" button.

By following these tips and leveraging the features available in PowerPoint, you can create and format slides that are visually engaging and effectively communicate your message. Remember to keep the design clean and uncluttered, use appropriate fonts and colors, and make good use of visuals and animations to enhance the presentation.

Adding and Editing Text on Slides

Text plays a crucial role in conveying your message on PowerPoint slides. Here are some steps to add and edit text on slides effectively:

1. **Adding text:** To add text to a slide, click on a text box or use the "Text Box" button in the Insert tab to create a new text box. You can also use existing placeholders on slide layouts. Once you have selected the text box or placeholder, start typing your text.

2. **Formatting text**: PowerPoint provides numerous options to format your text to make it visually appealing. After selecting the text, you can change the font, size, color, and alignment using the options in the Home tab's Font and Paragraph groups. You can also access additional formatting options, such as bold, italic, underline, strikethrough, and subscript/superscript.

3. **Applying text styles**: PowerPoint offers preset text styles that allow you to quickly apply consistent formatting to your text. In the Home tab, you'll find the "Styles" group, where you can choose from styles like Title, Subtitle, Heading, and so on. Applying these styles not only saves time but also helps maintain a consistent look throughout your presentation.

4. **Using bullets and numbering**: To create bulleted or numbered lists, select the text and click on the "Bullets" or "Numbering" button in the Home tab's Paragraph group. You can choose from various bullet styles or numbering formats. PowerPoint also allows you to customize the bullet points and numbering options.

5. **Adjusting line spacing and indentation:** PowerPoint gives you control over the line spacing and indentation of your text. To change the line spacing, select the text and go to the Home tab's Paragraph group. Use the "Line Spacing" options to increase or decrease the spacing. To adjust indentation, use the "Increase Indent" and "Decrease Indent" buttons.

6. **Adding hyperlinks**: You can make your text interactive by adding hyperlinks to other slides, websites, or files. Select the text you want to hyperlink and click on the "Hyperlink" button in the Insert tab. Choose the appropriate option, enter the URL or select the slide/file, and click "OK".

7. **Aligning and distributing text**: PowerPoint allows you to align text horizontally and vertically within text boxes or placeholders. Select the text and go to the Home tab's Paragraph group. Use the alignment buttons to align the text left, center, right, or justify. You can also use the "Align Text" options to distribute the text evenly within a text box or placeholder.

8. **Grouping and ungrouping text:** If you want to treat multiple text boxes or placeholders as a single unit, you can group them together. Simply select the text boxes or placeholders, right-click, and choose the "Group" option. To ungroup them, select the group, right-click, and select "Ungroup".

By following these steps, you can add and edit text effectively on your PowerPoint slides. Remember to keep your text concise, use appropriate fonts and formatting, and consider the readability of your text on the slide.

Formatting text using different font styles, sizes, colors, and effects

Formatting text is an essential aspect of creating visually appealing PowerPoint slides.

Here are some steps to format text using different font styles, sizes, colors, and effects:

1. **Select the text you want to format**: Click and drag the cursor over the text or use the Shift key and arrow keys to select multiple words or paragraphs.

2. **Changing font styles:** In the Home tab's Font group, you'll find the font style drop-down menu. Click on the arrow next to the font name to see the available options. Select the desired font style to apply it to the selected text. It's best to use clear and readable fonts.

3. **Adjusting font size**: In the same Font group, you'll find the font size drop-down menu. Click on the arrow and select the appropriate font size or type in a specific size. Alternatively, you can use the Increase Font Size or Decrease Font Size buttons to adjust the size incrementally.

4. **Changing font color**: To change the color of the selected text, click on the Font Color drop-down arrow in the Font group. You can choose from the preset colors or select "More Colors" to customize a specific shade. You can also use the Text Highlight Color option to highlight the text with a different color.

5. **Applying font effects**: PowerPoint offers various font effects to enhance your text. In the Font group, you'll find buttons for formatting options like bold, italic, underline, strikethrough, subscript, and superscript. Simply select the text and click on the desired effect button to apply or remove it.

6. **Combining font styles, sizes, and effects**: You can combine different font formatting options to create unique text styles. For example, you can have bold and italic text or underlined text with a different font color. Experimenting with different combinations can help you achieve the desired visual impact.

7. **Applying text effects**: PowerPoint also provides additional text effects, such as shadow, reflection, glow, and bevel. To access these effects, select the text and go to the Enhancements tab's WordArt Styles group. Click on the Text Effects button and choose the desired effect. This can add depth and visual interest to your text.

8. **Creating text outlines**: If you want to add an outline or border to your text, select the text and go to the Home tab's Font group. Click on the Text Outline button and choose the desired outline color, weight, or style. This can help make your text stand out against the background.

Remember to use text formatting consistently throughout your presentation to maintain a professional and cohesive look. Avoid excessive and unnecessary formatting, as it can distract from the main message. Regularly review your slides to ensure the text is readable and visually appealing.

Inserting and formatting images and shapes

Inserting and formatting images and shapes can enhance the visual appeal and overall design of your PowerPoint slides.

Here are steps to effectively insert and format images and shapes:

Inserting images:

1. Click on the "Insert" tab in the PowerPoint ribbon.

2. Click on the "Pictures" button to insert an image from your computer or the "Online Pictures" button to search for images on the web.

3. Select the image file you want to insert and click "Insert".

Formatting images:

1. Select the inserted image by clicking on it.

2. You can resize the image by clicking and dragging its corner handles.

3. To crop the image, click on the "Crop" button in the "Format" tab. Adjust the cropping handles to remove unwanted portions of the image.

4. You can also apply various picture styles, such as borders, shadows, and reflection effects, from the "Picture Styles" group in the "Format" tab.

Inserting shapes:

1. Click on the "Insert" tab in the PowerPoint ribbon.

2. In the "Illustrations" group, click on the "Shapes" button.

3. Choose the desired shape from the dropdown menu, such as rectangles, circles, arrows, etc.

4. Click and drag on the slide to create the shape.

Formatting shapes:

1. Select the shape by clicking on it.

2. To resize the shape, click and drag its corner handles.

3. You can change the fill color and outline color of the shape by using the options in the "Shape Styles" group in the "Format" tab.

4. The "Shape Fill" button allows you to choose solid colors, gradients, patterns, or even insert images as the shape fill.

5. The "Shape Outline" button enables you to modify the outline color, thickness, and style of the shape.

Grouping and arranging objects:

1. To group multiple objects together, select them by holding down the Shift key and clicking on each object. Right-click and choose "Group" from the context menu. This will merge the objects and allow them to be moved and formatted as a single unit.

2. To change the layering order, select the object and use the "Bring to Front", "Send to Back", or other options in the "Arrange" group of the "Format" tab.

By following these steps, you can effectively insert and format images and shapes in your PowerPoint slides. Remember to choose visually appealing images, use appropriate shapes to convey your message, and ensure that the formatting is consistent throughout your presentation.

Arranging and aligning elements on slides

Arranging and aligning elements on slides is crucial for creating a visually cohesive and professional-looking PowerPoint presentation.

Here are some tips for effectively arranging and aligning elements:

1. **Selecting multiple elements**: Hold down the Shift key and click on each element to select multiple objects at once.

2. **Aligning elements:**

☐ To align objects horizontally or vertically, select multiple objects and click on the "Align" button in the "Arrange" group of the "Format" tab. Choose options like "Align Top", "Align Center", or "Align Bottom" to align objects vertically. Similarly, choose options like "Align Left", "Align Center", or "Align Right" to align objects horizontally.

☐ You can also use the "Align to Slide" option to align objects relative to the entire slide.

3. **Distributing elements**:

☐ To distribute multiple objects evenly, select them, and click on the "Distribute" button in the "Arrange" group of the "Format" tab. Choose options such as "Distribute Horizontally" or "Distribute Vertically" to evenly space the selected objects.

4. **Grouping and ungrouping elements**:

☐ Grouping objects together allows you to move, format, and apply effects to them as a single unit. To group objects, select them, right-click, and choose "Group" from the context menu. You can also use the keyboard shortcut Ctrl+G.

☐ To ungroup objects, select the grouped objects, right-click, and choose "Ungroup" from the context menu. You can also use the keyboard shortcut Ctrl+Shift+G.

5. **Snap to grid:**

☐ Enabling the "Snap to Grid" option ensures that your objects align perfectly to a grid-based layout. To enable this feature, go to the "View" tab, click on the "Gridlines" button, and check the "Snap to Grid" option.

6. **Ordering and layering elements**:

☐ The "Arrange" group in the "Format" tab provides options for changing the layering order of objects. You can use commands like "Bring to Front", "Send to Back", "Bring Forward", or "Send Backward" to adjust the order in which objects appear.

By following these tips, you can arrange and align elements on your PowerPoint slides effectively, enhancing the overall visual organization and clarity of your presentation. Remember to review your slides for consistency in alignment, spacing, and grouping to ensure a professional and polished look.

Applying themes and slide backgrounds

Applying themes and slide backgrounds is an essential step in creating a visually appealing and cohesive PowerPoint presentation.

Follow these steps to apply themes and slide backgrounds to your presentation:

1. Open your PowerPoint presentation and navigate to the "Design" tab in the Ribbon at the top of the screen.

2. Explore the available themes by clicking on the thumbnails in the "Themes" gallery. Hovering over a theme will give you a live preview of how it will look on your slides.

3. Once you've selected a theme, PowerPoint will automatically apply it to all the slides in your presentation. Each theme consists of a set of coordinated colors, fonts, and effects that give your presentation a consistent and professional look.

4. If you want to change the background of a specific slide or a group of slides, select the slide(s) in the Slide Navigation pane on the left side of the screen.

5. With the slide(s) selected, go to the "Design" tab and click on the "Background" button in the "Customize" group. A drop-down menu will appear.

6. In the drop-down menu, choose from the available background options. You can select a solid color, gradient, picture, or pattern. PowerPoint provides pre-designed options, or you can browse for your own image by selecting "Picture or Texture Fill".

7. If you choose a picture or texture fill, you'll have the option to adjust the transparency, scale, and other settings to fit your needs.

8. After selecting the desired background option, click the "Apply to All" button if you want the background to apply to all slides, or click the "Apply" button to apply it only to the selected slide(s).

9. You can also apply a different theme to individual slides within your presentation by selecting the slide and then choosing a new theme from the "Themes" gallery. This allows for more flexibility and customization within your presentation.

By applying themes and slide backgrounds, you can quickly and easily give your PowerPoint presentation a professional and polished look.

Remember to choose a theme and background that align with the content and overall message of your presentation for the best visual impact.

Creating and Using Slide Master

Using Slide Masters in PowerPoint is a powerful way to ensure consistency and efficiency in creating and updating presentations. Slide Masters allow you to define and apply a consistent set of formatting elements, such as fonts, colors, backgrounds, and placeholders, to multiple slides at once

Creating a Slide Master in PowerPoint is a straightforward process that allows you to define the overall design and formatting for your presentation.

Follow these steps to create a Slide Master:

1. Open your PowerPoint presentation and navigate to the "View" tab in the Ribbon at the top of the screen.

2. In the "Presentation Views" group, click on "Slide Master". This will open the Slide Master view, displaying the Slide Master at the top, followed by the layouts associated with that master.

3. To create a new Slide Master, click on the "Insert Slide Master" button in the "Master Layout" group. A new Slide Master will appear in the layout pane.

4. To customize the Slide Master, you can modify various elements, such as:

    a. **Fonts**: Click on the "Fonts" button in the "Master Layout" group to select the desired font styles for your presentation.

    b. **Colors**: Click on the "Colors" button to choose a color scheme for your presentation or create a custom color palette.

    c. **Background**: Apply a background color, gradient, picture, or pattern to all slides by clicking on the "Background Styles" button.

    d. **Placeholders**: Adjust the position, size, and formatting of placeholders for text, images, charts, and other content elements on your slides.

5. Additionally, you can add elements like logos or headers to the Slide Master that will appear on every slide. To do this, simply select the desired layout or the Slide Master itself and insert the element.

6. To customize specific slide layouts, scroll down to the layout you want to modify and select it. Changes made to an individual layout will only affect slides using that layout.

7. Once you've finished customizing the Slide Master and layouts, you can exit the Slide Master view by clicking on the "Close Master View" button in the "Close" group on the Slide Master tab.

8. The changes you made in the Slide Master view will be applied to the rest of your presentation. To see the updated design on all slides, go back to the normal view by clicking on the "Normal" button in the "Presentation Views" group.

Creating and using a Slide Master allows you to establish a consistent look and feel for your presentation, making it easier to maintain and update. By designing and customizing the Slide Master, you can save time and ensure a professional look for your slides throughout the entire presentation.

Make sure to explore all the customization options available in the Slide Master view to create a visually appealing and cohesive presentation.

Modifying Slide Master layouts and designs

Modifying Slide Master layouts and designs allows you to further customize your presentation to meet your specific needs.

Here are the steps to modify Slide Master layouts and designs:

1. Open your PowerPoint presentation and switch to Slide Master view by clicking on the "View" tab in the Ribbon and selecting "Slide Master" in the "Presentation Views" group.

2. In the Slide Master view, you will see the Slide Master at the top, followed by the associated layouts below it.

3. To modify a layout, select the desired layout from the list of layouts. You can customize individual layouts by changing the font, colors, background, or placeholders for that specific layout.

4. To change the font of a layout, go to the "Slide Master" tab on the Ribbon and click on the "Fonts" button in the "Master Layout" group. Select the font styles you want to apply to the selected layout.

5. Customize the colors of the layout by clicking on the "Colors" button in the "Master Layout" group. Choose a pre-defined color scheme or create a custom color palette for the selected layout.

6. To change the background of a layout, click on the "Background Styles" button in the "Master Layout" group. You can apply a solid color, gradient, picture, or pattern to the background of the selected layout.

7. Adjust the placeholders for text, images, charts, and other content elements to suit your needs. You can resize, reposition, or format the placeholders by selecting them and using the formatting options available in the "Slide Master" tab.

8. If you want to make changes to the overall Slide Master design, you can modify the Slide Master itself. Select the Slide Master at the top of the Slide Master view and apply any desired changes to fonts, colors, backgrounds, or placeholders

9. Once you have made the desired modifications to the Slide Master layouts and designs, exit the Slide Master view by clicking on the "Close Master View" button in the "Close" group on the Slide Master tab.

10. The changes you made in the Slide Master view will be applied to all slides in your presentation that use those specific layouts. To see the updated designs on your slides, switch back to the normal view by clicking on the "Normal" button in the "Presentation Views" group.

Modifying Slide Master layouts and designs allows you to create a consistent and visually appealing presentation. By customizing individual layouts and the overall Slide Master, you can have full control over the design elements of your slides and ensure a professional and cohesive look throughout your presentation.

Applying Slide Master to create consistent slide formatting throughout the presentation

Applying Slide Master to create consistent slide formatting throughout the presentation ensures a professional and cohesive look.

Here are the steps to apply Slide Master:

1. Open your PowerPoint presentation and go to the "View" tab in the Ribbon.

2. Click on "Slide Master" in the "Presentation Views" group. This will open the Slide Master view.

3. In the Slide Master view, you will see the Slide Master at the top, followed by the associated layouts below it.

4. To apply the Slide Master to all slides in your presentation, make any desired formatting changes to the Slide Master itself. For example, you can change the font, colors, backgrounds, or placeholders.

5. The changes you make in the Slide Master will be automatically applied to all slides that use that specific Slide Master and its layouts.

6. To customize individual layouts, select the desired layout from the list of layouts in the Slide Master view. Make any necessary changes like adjusting placeholders or formatting elements.

7. You can also add new layouts to your Slide Master by right-clicking on an existing layout and selecting "Insert Layout". This enables you to have different formatting options for specific slides in your presentation.

8. Once you have made all the desired modifications to the Slide Master and layouts, exit the Slide Master view by clicking on the "Close Master View" button in the "Close" group on the Slide Master tab.

9. In the normal view, you will see that all your slides now have the consistent formatting applied from the Slide Master.

By applying Slide Master, you can easily create consistent slide formatting throughout your entire presentation. This saves time by avoiding the need to manually format each slide individually. It also ensures that your presentation looks polished and professional, with a cohesive design that aligns with your branding or specific style requirements.

Enhancing Slides with Graphics and Media

Enhancing slides with graphics and media can make your presentation more engaging and visually appealing.
Here are some tips on how to effectively use graphics and media in your slides:

1. **Images**: Adding relevant images can help illustrate your points and grab the audience's attention. Choose high-quality images that are clear and visually appealing. You can use stock photos or your own original images. To add an image, click on the "Insert" tab in the Ribbon, select "Pictures," and choose the image file from your computer. Resize and position the image as desired.

2. **Charts and Graphs**: Use charts and graphs to present data and statistics in a visually appealing and easy-to-understand way. PowerPoint provides various chart options that you can customize to suit your needs. To add a chart, click on the "Insert" tab, select "Chart," and choose the chart type you want to use. Enter your data in the Excel spreadsheet that appears, and customize the chart's formatting as needed.

3. **Videos**: Incorporating videos into your slides can be a powerful way to convey information or demonstrate a process. Ensure the video file is compatible with PowerPoint (usually MP4 or WMV format), and insert it by clicking on the "Insert" tab, selecting "Video," and choosing the video file from your computer. You can resize and position the video, and set options such as playing automatically or on click.

4. **Audio**: Adding audio to your slides can be effective for including narration, sound effects, or background music. Insert audio by clicking on the "Insert" tab, selecting "Audio," and choosing the audio file. Set options such as playing automatically or on click, and adjust volume levels as needed. Test the audio playback to ensure it works correctly on the presentation platform.

5. **Animations and Transitions**: Use animations and transitions to add movement and visual interest to your slides. Apply animations to individual objects or text elements by selecting them and clicking on the "Animations" tab. Transitions control how slides appear and disappear during a slideshow. Click on the "Transitions" tab to choose a desired transition effect or modify the duration and timing.

6. **Captions and Labels**: To provide additional context or explain graphics and media, consider using captions or labels. You can add text boxes with descriptive labels or use PowerPoint's built-in caption feature for images. Ensure that the captions and labels are clear, concise, and properly positioned to support the visuals without overwhelming them.

Remember to use graphics and media sparingly and purposefully. They should enhance your presentation and support your message, rather than distract or overwhelm the audience. Use them strategically to make your slides visually appealing, engaging, and effective in conveying information.

Inserting and Formatting Tables, Charts, and SmartArt Graphics

Inserting and formatting tables, charts, and SmartArt graphics can help you display data and information in an organized and visually appealing way.

Here are some tips on how to effectively use these elements in your presentation:

Tables:

1. To insert a table, click on the "Insert" tab in the Ribbon, select "Table," and choose the number of rows and columns you need.

2. Once the table is inserted, click inside a cell to enter text or data. You can navigate through the cells using the tab key or arrow keys.

3. Format the table by selecting it and using the Table Tools Design and Layout tabs that appear in the Ribbon. Here, you can change the table style, adjust the cell borders and spacing, and apply shading or colors to the cells.

Charts:

1. To insert a chart, click on the "Insert" tab in the Ribbon, select "Chart," and choose the desired chart type from the options available (such as column, bar, pie, line, etc.).

2. A linked Excel sheet will open where you can enter your data or copy and paste it from another source. The chart will automatically update to reflect the changes in the linked data.

3. Customize the chart using the Chart Tools Design and Format tabs that appear in the Ribbon. Here, you can change the chart style, colors, labels, axes, and add data labels or titles.

SmartArt graphics:

SmartArt graphics are pre-designed visual representations of different concepts, such as processes, hierarchies, cycles, or relationship diagrams.

1. To insert a SmartArt graphic, click on the "Insert" tab in the Ribbon, select "SmartArt," and choose a category and layout that suits your needs.

2. Click on the placeholder text in the graphic to replace it with your own text or click on the "+" icon to add more shapes or levels.

3. Format the SmartArt graphic using the SmartArt Tools Design and Format tabs that appear in the Ribbon. Here, you can change the color, style, layout, and add effects or animations to the graphic.

Remember to keep your tables, charts, and SmartArt graphics simple, clear, and easy to understand. Use appropriate colors, fonts, and labels to make the information visually appealing and accessible to your audience. Avoid cluttering the visuals with excessive text or data and ensure that they are in line with the overall design and theme of your presentation.

Adding and Editing Audio and Video Content

Adding and editing audio and video content to your presentation can enhance the engagement and impact of your message.

Here are some guidelines on how to effectively incorporate audio and video into your PowerPoint slides:

Adding Audio:

1. To add audio, click on the "Insert" tab in the Ribbon, select "Audio," and choose whether to insert an audio file from your computer or an online source.

2. Once inserted, the audio file appears as an icon on the slide. You can move and resize it as needed.

3. Customize the audio playback options by selecting the audio icon and using the Audio Tools Playback tab that appears in the Ribbon. Here, you can set the audio to play automatically or on click, adjust the volume, and control other settings.

4. Test the audio playback to ensure that it works as intended on the presentation platform.

Editing Audio:

1. To edit audio, click on the audio icon and select the Audio Tools Playback tab in the Ribbon. Here, you can trim the audio to remove unwanted portions or adjust the start and end times.

2. You can also apply effects, such as fade in/out, volume adjustments, or add bookmarks to specific sections of the audio. Use the Audio Tools Playback tab to access these editing options.

Adding Video:

1. To add a video, click on the "Insert" tab in the Ribbon, select "Video," and choose whether to insert a video file from your computer or an online source.

2. Once inserted, the video appears as a placeholder on the slide. You can move, resize, and reposition it as desired.

3. Customize the video playback options by selecting the video placeholder and using the Video Tools Playback tab that appears in the Ribbon. Here, you can set the video to play automatically or on click, adjust the volume, and control other settings.

4. You can also set a poster frame, which is the static image that appears before the video is played, by right-clicking on the video and selecting "Set Poster Frame."

Editing Video:

1. PowerPoint offers basic video editing capabilities. Right-click on the video, select "Edit Video," and you can trim the video to remove unwanted sections.

2. You can also apply video styles, such as adding borders or adjusting the brightness or contrast. Use the Video Tools Format tab to access these editing options.

3. Keep in mind that PowerPoint's video editing features are limited compared to professional video editing software. Consider using external video editing tools for more advanced editing requirements.

Remember to optimize your audio and video files for PowerPoint by using compatible formats (such as MP3 or MP4), compressing them if necessary to reduce file size, and ensuring the files are stored in the same location as your presentation to avoid playback issues. Test the playback of audio and video content on the intended presentation platform to ensure a smooth experience for your audience.

Using Transitions and Animations to Enhance Slide Transitions and Object Appearances

Using transitions and animations in your PowerPoint presentation can enhance the flow of information and engage your audience.

Here are some tips on how to effectively utilize transitions and animations to enhance slide transitions and object appearances:

Transitions between slides:

1. To apply a slide transition, click on the "Transitions" tab in the Ribbon. You can choose from various transition options, such as fades, blinds, flips, or zooms.

2. Select the transition style you want to apply by clicking on it. You can preview the effect by clicking the "Preview" button before applying it to the entire presentation.

3. Customize the transition settings by adjusting the duration (how long the transition takes), applying sound effects, or choosing to advance the slide on mouse-click or automatically after a specified time.

4. Consider using subtle and professional transitions that complement your presentation content. Avoid excessive or flashy transitions that may distract from your message.

Animations on objects:

1. To apply animations to objects, select the object you want to animate, and click on the "Animations" tab in the Ribbon.

2. Choose an animation effect from the available options, such as entrance, exit, emphasis, or motion paths.

3. You can further customize the animation by selecting options like the direction, duration, and timing of the animation.

4. Use animations strategically to draw attention to important points or to reveal information gradually. Animated charts or diagrams can help explain complex concepts in a step-by-step manner.

5. Avoid overusing animations, as they can become distracting if used excessively. Stick to a consistent animation style throughout your presentation to maintain a professional look.

Animation sequence and timing:

1. To control the sequence and timing of animations, use the "Animation Pane" on the Animations tab. The Animation Pane allows you to manage and reorder animations on objects.

2. By default, animations are triggered on mouse-click. However, you can adjust the start of animations to occur on mouse-click, with a previous animation, or after a specified delay.

3. Consider the flow of information on your slides and use animation timings to control when and how objects appear. This can help guide the audience's focus and comprehension.

4. Practice your presentation with animations to ensure that they are synchronized correctly and add value to your message.

Remember, when using transitions and animations, it's important to strike a balance between engaging your audience and maintaining professionalism. Overusing effects can distract from your content, while using them sparingly and purposefully can enhance the visual appeal and delivery of your presentation. Always consider the preferences and expectations of your audience and tailor your use of transitions and animations accordingly.

Creating Effective Slide Content

Creating effective slide content is crucial for delivering a successful presentation. Here are some tips for creating engaging and impactful slide content:

1. **Keep it simple**: Avoid cluttering your slides with too much text or excessive visuals. Stick to the main points and use concise sentences or bullet points. This makes it easier for your audience to read and understand the information.

2. **Use visuals**: Visuals, such as images, graphs, charts, or diagrams, can help convey information more effectively than text alone. Use visuals to support your key points and make the content more engaging and memorable.

3. **Limit text:** Use text sparingly and only include essential information on each slide. Long paragraphs or excessive bullet points can overwhelm your audience and lead to information overload. Use short phrases or keywords that summarize the main ideas.

4. **Maintain consistency**: Use a consistent design throughout your presentation to create a professional and cohesive look. Stick to a single font, color scheme, and style. This helps your audience focus on the content without getting distracted by inconsistent visuals.

5. **Use appropriate font size:** Ensure that your text is large enough to be easily read from a distance. A font size of at least 24 points is recommended for body text, while a larger font size should be used for headings or important points.

6. **Use clear and legible fonts**: Choose fonts that are easy to read, even from a distance. Sans-serif fonts like Arial or Calibri are commonly used for body text, while bold or decorative fonts can be used for headings or titles sparingly.

7. **Use a logical flow**: Organize your slides in a logical manner to guide your audience through the content. Use clear headings and subheadings to indicate the flow of information. Consider using transition slides to introduce new sections or topics.

8. **Create visually appealing slides**: Pay attention to the overall design and aesthetic of your slides. Use white space effectively to give your content room to breathe. Balance text and visuals, and use colors that are visually pleasing and complement your topic.

9. **Use animations and transitions strategically:** As mentioned earlier, animations and transitions can enhance the flow of information and engage your audience. Use them selectively to highlight key points or to reveal information gradually, but avoid excessive or distracting effects.

10. **Proofread and edit**: Always proofread your slides for any spelling or grammatical errors. Ensure that all information is accurate and up to date. Edit your content to ensure it is concise and focused on the main message you want to convey.

By following these tips, you can create slides that effectively communicate your message, engage your audience, and enhance the overall impact of your presentation. Remember to practice your presentation and make necessary adjustments to fine-tune your slide content for maximum effectiveness.

Designing Clear and Concise Slide Content

Designing clear and concise slide content is crucial for delivering an impactful and engaging presentation.
Here are some tips to help you create slides that effectively communicate your message:

1. **Focus on key points**: Your slides should only include the most important information. Identify the key messages you want to convey and eliminate any irrelevant or extraneous content. This will make your slides more focused and easier for your audience to follow.

2. **Use concise and clear language:** Avoid using long paragraphs or complex sentences on your slides. Use short phrases, bullet points, or keywords to convey your main ideas. This helps your audience to easily understand and remember the information.

3. **Limit the amount of text**: Slide content should be brief and to the point. Avoid overcrowding your slides with excessive text. Stick to one main point per slide and use visuals or diagrams to supplement or illustrate your message.

4. **Utilize visuals effectively**: Visuals, such as images, graphs, or charts, can help convey information more efficiently than text alone. Use visuals that support your key points and make them visually appealing. Always ensure that the visuals are clear and communicate the intended message.

5. **Maintain consistency in design**: Choose a consistent design and layout for your slides. Use the same font type and size throughout the presentation. Keep the color scheme and formatting consistent to create a cohesive and professional look.

6. **Use appropriate font size**: Make sure the text on your slides is easily readable from a distance. Use a font size of at least 24 points for body text, and a larger font size for headings or important points. This ensures that your audience can read the content without straining.

7. **Organize content logically**: Arrange your slides in a logical sequence that flows smoothly. Use clear headings and subheadings to guide your audience through the information. Consider using a table of contents slide or section dividers to help your audience navigate the presentation.

8. **Minimize distractions**: Avoid clutter on your slides and eliminate any unnecessary elements that can distract your audience. Keep the focus on the main message by removing any non-essential information or excessive visual effects.

9. **Review and edit**: Before finalizing your slides, review and edit the content for clarity and conciseness. Proofread for any spelling or grammatical errors. Make sure that each slide contributes to the overall flow and narrative of your presentation.

10. **Practice and refine**: Practice your presentation with the slides to ensure that the content flows smoothly and that you can present it confidently. Make any necessary adjustments or improvements to the slide content based on your practice sessions.

By designing clear and concise slide content, you can effectively communicate your message, engage your audience, and deliver a successful presentation. Remember to keep the focus on the key points and use visuals and language that are easy to understand and remember.

Using Bullet Points, Numbering, and Indentation Effectively

Bullet points, numbering, and indentation are formatting tools which can effectively enhance the clarity and organization of your slide content.

Here are some tips on how to use these formatting tools effectively:

Bullet points:

1. Use bullet points to list multiple items or concepts.

2. Keep each bullet point concise, using short phrases or keywords.

3. Use parallel structure, keeping the format consistent for each bullet point.

4. Use bullet points to highlight key ideas or key supporting details.

5. Limit the number of bullet points per slide to maintain readability and prevent overload.

Numbering:

1. Use numbering to indicate a specific order or sequence.

2. Use numbers for steps in a process, key points in a list, or any other sequential information.

3. Make sure to order the numbers logically and clearly.

4. When using numbers, consider using a sublevel, such as 1.1, 1.2, etc., to indicate a subcategory or subsection.

Indentation:

1. Utilize indentation to show relationships and hierarchy.

2. Use indentation to create sub-points or subordinate ideas within a main point.

3. Indentation helps visually separate main ideas from supporting details.

4. Use consistent and meaningful indentation throughout your slides to maintain clarity.

Moreso, bullet points, numbering, and indentation can help break up information into more manageable chunks, making it easier for your audience to follow along and understand. By using these formatting techniques effectively, you can create visually appealing slides that communicate your message clearly and concisely.

Incorporating Visuals and Multimedia Appropriately

Visuals and multimedia can greatly enhance the effectiveness and engagement of your presentation.
Here are some tips on how to incorporate visuals and multimedia effectively:

1. **Choose relevant visuals**: Select visuals, such as images, graphs, charts, or videos, that directly support and enhance your key message. Ensure that the visuals are relevant to the content and help illustrate or emphasize your points.

2. **Keep visuals simple and clear**: Avoid using visuals that are overly complex or cluttered. Use visuals that have a clear focus and are easy to understand. If using graphs or charts, make sure the data is presented clearly and can be easily interpreted.

3. **Use high-quality visuals**: Use high-resolution images and clear graphics to ensure that the visuals are visually appealing and easily visible on the screen. Poor quality visuals can distract or confuse your audience.

4. **Incorporate multimedia strategically**: Use multimedia elements, such as videos, audio clips, or animations, to enhance and illustrate your message. However, ensure that the multimedia elements are relevant, add value to your presentation, and do not distract from your main points.

5. **Time multimedia appropriately**: If incorporating videos or audio clips, make sure they are timed appropriately and align with your presentation flow. Avoid lengthy multimedia that may take up too much time or disrupt the flow of your presentation.

6. **Provide context for visuals**: When presenting visuals, provide a brief explanation or context to help your audience understand the significance of the visual and how it relates to your message. This will help your audience interpret the visual correctly.

7. **Test and prepare multimedia in advance:** Prior to your presentation, test all multimedia elements to ensure they work properly and are compatible with the presentation software and equipment. Make sure you have backup options in case of technical difficulties.

8. **Use multimedia sparingly**: While multimedia can be engaging, use it judiciously to avoid overwhelming or distracting your audience. Only include multimedia elements that add value and align with your presentation objectives.

9. **Consider accessibility**: When using visuals or multimedia, consider the accessibility needs of your audience. Provide alternative ways to convey the information, such as providing captions for videos or providing alternative text for images.

10. **Practice with visuals and multimedia:** Practice your presentation with the visuals and multimedia to ensure they integrate smoothly and seamlessly into your delivery. Familiarize yourself with any timing or cues related to the multimedia elements.

By incorporating visuals and multimedia appropriately, you can enhance the impact and engagement of your presentation. Visuals and multimedia can help reinforce your message, make it more memorable, and cater to different learning styles. Remember to choose visuals and multimedia that are relevant, clear, and supportive of your main points.

Applying Consistent Formatting and Design Principles

Applying consistent formatting and design principles to your presentation is crucial for creating a polished and professional look.

Here are some tips to help you maintain consistency in your formatting and design:

1. **Choose a consistent color scheme**: Select a color scheme that aligns with your content and purpose. Stick to a limited number of colors and apply them consistently throughout your slides. This will create a cohesive and visually appealing presentation.

2. **Use consistent fonts**: Select a font or a set of fonts that are easy to read and convey your message effectively. Stick to one or two fonts throughout your presentation to maintain consistency. Ensure that the font sizes are consistent as well, to maintain visual harmony.

3. **Establish a consistent layout**: Create a template or master slide that establishes the layout for your presentation. This layout should include elements such as headers, text boxes, image placeholders, and bullet point styles. This will help maintain a consistent structure across your slides.

4. **Align elements consistently**: Pay attention to the alignment of text, images, and other visual elements. Use a grid or a guide to align elements consistently within your slides. This will give your presentation a clean and organized appearance.

5. **Apply consistent formatting to text:** Use consistent formatting for headings, subheadings, body text, and other text elements. This includes font styles, font sizes, and text formatting such as bold, italics, or underline. Consistent formatting will make your text look professional and easy to read.

6. **Use consistent image styles:** If you include images in your presentation, consider using consistent styles for how they are presented. This could

include applying borders, shapes, or filters to images. Consistency in image styles will tie your visuals together and create a cohesive visual theme.

7. **Maintain consistent slide transitions**: If you choose to use slide transitions, apply them consistently throughout your presentation. Stick to one or two transition styles to avoid a jarring or inconsistent experience for your audience.

8. **Balance white space**: White space, or empty space, plays an important role in design. Ensure that your slides are not overly cluttered with text or visuals. Use white space effectively to create visual breathing room and make your content easier to digest.

9. **Consider branding guidelines**: If you are creating a presentation for a specific organization or brand, follow their branding guidelines. Incorporate logos, colors, fonts, and other visual elements that align with the brand's identity.

10. **Proofread and edit consistently**: Consistency extends beyond design principles. It is important to make sure your content is error-free and consistent in terms of grammar, punctuation, and formatting. Proofread and edit your presentation meticulously to ensure consistency in your written content as well.

By applying consistent formatting and design principles, you not only create a visually pleasing presentation but also demonstrate professionalism and attention to detail. Consistency helps your audience focus on the content and message rather than being distracted by inconsistent or haphazard design choices. Take the time to establish a consistent visual identity for your presentation, and it will greatly enhance its overall effectiveness.

Creating and Presenting Slide Shows

This is a powerful tool for sharing information and engaging your audience.
Here are some tips to help you create and deliver effective slide shows:

1. **Define your objective**: Before you start creating your slides, clarify the purpose and objective of your presentation. What message do you want to convey, and what do you want your audience to take away from it? This will help you structure your content and ensure that every slide contributes to your main objective.

2. **Keep it simple**: Avoid overcrowding your slides with too much information. Stick to one main idea per slide and use bullet points or concise phrases to convey your message. Too much text can overwhelm your audience and make it harder for them to follow along.

3. **Use visuals wisely**: Incorporate relevant and engaging visuals, such as images, charts, graphs, or diagrams, to enhance your message and make it more memorable. Choose high-quality visuals that are easy to understand and support your content. Be sure to credit the source of any borrowed images or graphics.

4. **Design with consistency**: Apply the principles of consistency mentioned earlier to your slide design. Consistent fonts, color schemes, and layouts will not only make your slides look polished but also help your audience follow along more easily. Avoid using too many different fonts or colors that may distract from your message.

5. **Use animations and transitions sparingly**: While animations and slide transitions can add visual interest to your presentation, use them sparingly and strategically. Too many animations or rapid transitions can be distracting and take away from the content. Use them to emphasize important points or reveal information gradually, enhancing engagement and comprehension.

6. **Practice and time your presentation**: Rehearse your presentation multiple times before delivering it to ensure you are familiar with your slides and comfortable with the flow of the content. Pay attention to your timing and make sure you are within the allotted time. Practice will also help you become more confident and smooth in delivering your presentation.

7. **Engage with your audience**: During your presentation, make an effort to connect with your audience. Maintain eye contact, speak clearly and confidently, and use body language to engage your listeners. Encourage questions and interaction to keep the audience involved and interested.

8. **Use speaker notes:** Prepare speaker notes or a script to guide you through your presentation. These can serve as reminders for important points, transitions, and cues for timing. Speaker notes will help you stay on track and deliver a clear and organized presentation.

9. **Seek feedback and make improvements**: After your presentation, ask for feedback from trusted colleagues or audience members. This feedback will help you identify areas for improvement, such as content clarity or slide design. Use this feedback to refine your slide show for future presentations.

10. **Continuously evaluate and update your slides**: As you gain more experience and feedback from delivering slide shows, be open to refining and updating your slides. Stay current with the content, visuals, and design trends, and adapt your slides accordingly for maximum impact.

By following these tips, you can create and deliver slide shows that effectively communicate your message, engage your audience, and leave a lasting impression. The key is to keep your slides concise, visually appealing, and well-structured, while also maintaining a confident and engaging delivery.

Setting Slide Show Options, such as Slide Timings and Transitions

Setting slide show options, such as slide timings and transitions, is an important step in creating an engaging and professional presentation. These options can add visual interest and help to control the flow of information during your slide show. Here are some tips on how to set up these options effectively:

1. **Slide Timings**: Slide timings are useful when you want your slides to progress automatically, whether you are presenting in person or recording your presentation to share later. To set slide timings, follow these steps:

   A. Open your presentation in the slide show view.

   B. Click on the "Slide Show" tab in the ribbon.

   C. Click on "Set Up Slide Show" in the "Set Up" group.

   D. In the pop-up window, under the "Show type" section, select "Presented by a speaker (full screen)."

   E. Tick the box next to "Use timings, if present" under the "Advance slides" section.

   F. Click OK to save your settings.

   G. You can also manually set timings for individual slides by going to the "Transitions" tab and adjusting the "After" time in the "Timing" section.

2. Transitions: Slide transitions control the visual effects that occur when moving from one slide to the next. They can help to create smooth transitions and make your presentation appear more polished.
To set slide transitions, follow these steps:

A. Open your presentation in the slide show view.

B. Click on the "Transitions" tab in the ribbon.

C. Select the slide you want to apply a transition to.

D. Choose a desired transition from the available options in the "Transition to This Slide" group.

E. Use the "Effect Options" drop-down menu to further customize the transition, such as the direction or speed.

F. Click "Apply to All" if you want the same transition to be applied to all the slides in your presentation.

G. Preview your transitions by selecting "Preview" in the "Preview" group. This will allow you to see how the transitions look in your presentation.

Remember to use transitions sparingly and choose those that align with the content and tone of your presentation. Overusing or using distracting transitions may hinder rather than enhance the overall message.

3. Animations: In addition to slide transitions, you can also use animations to add movement and visual interest to individual objects on your slides. Animations can be applied to text, images, charts, and other elements.
To set animations:

A. Select the object you want to animate.

B. Go to the "Animations" tab in the ribbon.

C. Choose an animation effect from the available options in the "Animation" group.

D. Customize the animation options, such as duration or delay, using the tools in the "Timing" and "Advanced Animation" groups.

E. Preview the animation by selecting "Preview" in the "Preview" group.

F. Like transitions, use animations sparingly and purposefully. Be mindful that the animations do not distract from the content but enhance it.

Remember, when using slide timings, transitions, and animations, it's important to strike a balance between engaging your audience and avoiding distracting them from the main content. By setting up these options effectively and thoughtfully, you can create a visually captivating slide show that enhances your presentation.

Rehearsing and Delivering Presentations Effectively

Rehearsing and delivering presentations effectively is crucial for engaging your audience, conveying your message clearly, and boosting your overall confidence. Here are some tips to help you rehearse and deliver presentations effectively:

1. **Prepare and Organize**: Start by thoroughly researching your topic and organizing your content in a logical and coherent manner. Create an outline or structure for your presentation, including an introduction, main points, and conclusion. Make sure your content flows smoothly and supports your main message.

2. **Practice, Practice, Practice**: Rehearsing your presentation is key to delivering it effectively. Practice out loud, preferably in front of a mirror or with a friend or colleague who can provide feedback. This will help you become familiar with your material, improve your delivery, and identify areas that need improvement.

3. **Time Yourself**: Pay attention to your timing during practice sessions. Aim to stay within the allotted time or the time recommended for your presentation. This will help you pace yourself and ensure that you cover all the important points without rushing or dragging on.

4. **Use Visual Aids**: If appropriate, incorporate visual aids such as PowerPoint slides, charts, or diagrams to enhance your presentation. Ensure that your visual aids are clear, visually appealing, and support your key points. Practice using them and familiarize yourself with any technical equipment or software you'll be using.

5. **Speak Clearly and Confidently**: Focus on speaking clearly and confidently during your presentation. Articulate your words, vary your tone and pace, and project your voice so that everyone in the room can hear you. Avoid mumbling or speaking too quickly. Work on developing a confident posture and body language to establish your credibility and engage your audience.

6. **Engage Your Audience**: Maintain good eye contact with your audience and try to establish a connection. Be aware of their reactions and adjust your delivery accordingly. Encourage participation through questions, polls, or interactive activities, if appropriate.

7. **Handle Questions and Challenges**: Anticipate potential questions or challenges that might arise and prepare thoughtful and concise responses. During your practice sessions, have someone play the role of the audience and ask questions or provide feedback to help you refine your answers.

8. **Seek Feedback**: Request feedback from trusted individuals who can give you constructive criticism on your delivery, content, and overall presentation skills. Use this feedback to make necessary improvements and adjustments.

9. **Record Yourself**: Consider recording yourself during one of your practice sessions. This will allow you to review your performance objectively and identify areas for improvement, such as vocal clarity, body language, or pace.

10. **Reflect and Learn**: After delivering your presentation, take the time to reflect on your performance. Identify what worked well and what you can improve for future presentations. Continually seek opportunities to enhance your presentation skills through practice and feedback.

Remember, effective rehearsing and delivering presentations requires planning, practice, and continuous improvement. By implementing these tips, you can boost your presentation skills and deliver engaging and impactful presentations.

Customizing SlideShow Navigation and Interaction

Customizing slideshow navigation and interaction can greatly enhance your presentation and engage your audience.

Here are some tips to help you tailor your slideshow navigation and interaction:

1. **Use a Consistent and Intuitive Layout**: Design a clear and consistent navigation layout for your slides. Consider using a menu or navigation bar that allows users to easily move between slides or sections. Make sure the layout is intuitive and doesn't confuse the audience.

2. **Customize Slide Transitions**: Instead of using default slide transitions, customize them to match the theme and tone of your presentation. Select transitions that are subtle and not distracting. Use transitions to smoothly guide your audience from one slide to another.

3. **Insert Hyperlinks**: Hyperlinks can be a powerful tool to enhance interactivity in your slide show. You can insert hyperlinks to external websites, documents, or other slides within your presentation. This allows you to provide additional information or direct the audience to relevant resources.

4. **Incorporate Interactive Elements**: Consider adding interactive elements to your slides, such as quizzes, polls, or clickable icons. These elements can actively involve the audience and create a more engaging and memorable experience. Make sure the interactive elements are relevant to your presentation and effectively support your message.

5. **Utilize Animation Effects**: Animation effects can be used to highlight key points, reveal information gradually, or add visual interest to your slides. Customizing animation effects can make your presentation more dynamic and attention-grabbing. However, use animations sparingly and ensure they enhance rather than distract from your content.

6. **Enable Slide Zoom**: Modern presentation software like PowerPoint allows you to enable slide zoom, which allows you to zoom in on specific areas or details of a slide during your presentation. This can be useful for emphasizing important points or showcasing visuals with more clarity.

7. **Provide Navigation Tips**: If your slide show has complex navigation or interactive elements, consider providing clear instructions or navigation tips at the beginning of your presentation. This will help the audience understand how to interact with your slides and make the most of the interactive features.

8. **Test and Rehearse**: Before presenting, thoroughly test and rehearse your slide show navigation and interactive elements. Ensure that all hyperlinks, animations, and interactive elements work as intended. Seek feedback from others to ensure your navigation is easy to follow and the interactive elements are effective.

9. **Keep Accessibility in Mind**: Consider the accessibility of your slide show when customizing navigation and interaction. Ensure that your navigation is accessible to everyone, including those with visual or motor impairments. Use alt text for images, provide captions or transcripts for audio or video elements, and ensure good color contrast.

10. **Review and Update**: After delivering your presentation, take the time to review and update your slide show navigation and interaction based on feedback and your own observations. Continuously improving and refining your navigation and interaction will help you deliver more impactful and engaging presentations.

Customizing slideshow navigation and interaction allows you to create a tailored and interactive experience for your audience. By following these tips, you can make your presentations more engaging, memorable, and effective.

Printing and Distributing Presentations

Printing and distributing presentations can be a convenient way to provide your audience with physical copies of your slides. Here are some tips to consider when printing and distributing presentations:

1. **Determine the Purpose**: Before printing and distributing your presentation, determine the purpose for providing physical copies. Are they meant to be a reference guide, handout during the presentation, or for distribution after the presentation? This will help you decide what content to include and how to format the handout.

2. **Simplify and Condense**: When printing slides, it's important to simplify and condense the content. Remove excessive text and keep the visuals and key points. Remember, the printed handout shouldn't replace your presentation, but rather serve as a complement.

3. **Choose the Right Layout**: Consider the layout of your handout. You can opt for a traditional slide layout, with one slide per page, or choose a more condensed layout with multiple slides per page. Experiment with different layouts to find what works best for your presentation.

4. **Include Additional Information:** Depending on the purpose of the handout, you may want to include additional information like references, sources, or supplemental content. This can provide your audience with more detailed information and resources to explore.

5. **Use Adequate Font Sizes:** Ensure that the text on your handouts is legible. Use a font size that is easy to read, considering that the handout will likely be smaller than the projected slides. Additionally, choose fonts that are clear and professional-looking.

6. **Check for Consistency**: Double-check that your handouts are consistent with your digital slides. Make sure that the fonts, colors, and overall design align with your presentation. Consistency will help reinforce your branding and provide a seamless experience for your audience.

7. **Print Quality:** When printing your presentations, use high-quality printing settings to ensure that the handouts come out clear and crisp. Consider using a professional printing service if needed to achieve the best results.

8. **Distribute Strategically**: Determine the best time and method to distribute your handouts. If you're providing them before the presentation, ensure that they won't distract the audience from your live presentation. If distributing after the presentation, make sure they are easily accessible and readily available.

9. **Consider Digital Alternatives**: In addition to printed handouts, you may also want to provide digital copies of your presentation. This can be done through email, file sharing services, or by uploading it to a website or online platform. Digital copies are convenient, easily shareable, and environmentally friendly.

10. **Collect Feedback**: After distributing your handouts, collect feedback from your audience. This will help you understand how effective the printed materials were and if any improvements can be made for future presentations.

Printing and distributing presentations can be an effective way to enhance your audience's experience and provide them with valuable resources. By following these tips, you can ensure that your printed handouts are clear, concise, and align with your overall presentation goals.

Advanced Presentation Techniques

Advanced presentation techniques can take your presentations to the next level, making them more engaging, impactful, and memorable. Here are some advanced presentation techniques to consider incorporating into your presentations:

1. **Storytelling**: One of the most powerful techniques is storytelling. By incorporating relevant and compelling stories into your presentation, you can capture the attention of your audience and make your key messages resonate with them on a deeper level. Use personal anecdotes, case studies, or narratives that illustrate your points and evoke emotions.

2. **Visuals and Multimedia**: Enhance your presentations by incorporating captivating visuals and multimedia elements. Use high-quality images, videos, infographics, or animations to support your content and make it more visually appealing. This can help in conveying complex information or creating a memorable impact.

3. **Interactivity**: Engage your audience by incorporating interactive elements into your presentation. This can include activities, quizzes, polls, or group discussions. By involving your audience actively, you can increase their participation and create a more dynamic and memorable experience.

4. **Audience-Centric Approach**: Tailor your presentation to your specific audience. Research their needs, interests, and preferences beforehand to ensure that your content and delivery style resonate with them. Address their pain points, solve their problems, and provide value that is relevant to their concerns.

5. **Emotional Appeals**: Connect with your audience on an emotional level by appealing to their emotions. Use heartfelt stories, impactful visuals, or persuasive language that evokes specific emotions such as joy, empathy, excitement, or inspiration. Emotionally charged presentations are more likely to be remembered and create a lasting impact.

6. **Advanced Visual Design**: Pay attention to the visual design of your presentation slides. Use consistent branding, choose attractive fonts and colors, and optimize the layout to be visually appealing. Keep the design clean and uncluttered, ensuring that the visual elements enhance the content rather than distracting from it.

7. **Non-Linear Presentations**: Break away from the traditional linear presentation format by using non-linear approaches. Non-linear presentations allow you to navigate freely between topics or slides, enabling you to adapt the flow based on audience feedback, questions, or interests. This interactive approach can make your presentation more dynamic and engaging.

8. **Engaging Opening and Closing**: Grab your audience's attention right from the start with a captivating opening. Use a powerful quote, a thought-provoking question, or an intriguing story to immediately capture their interest. Similarly, close your presentation with a strong and memorable ending. Summarize the key points, leave them with a call-to-action, or end with a compelling story or quote that reinforces your message.

9. **Rehearse and Refine**: Practice your presentation thoroughly to ensure a smooth delivery. Rehearse your content, timing, and transitions to build confidence and ensure that you're able to deliver your message effectively. Pay attention to your body language, voice modulation, and pacing to engage your audience and maintain their interest.

10. **Use Technology Effectively**: Leverage technology and presentation tools to enhance your delivery. Use features like animation, slide transitions, or

interactive software to create a visually dynamic and engaging experience. However, use technology judiciously, ensuring that it enhances rather than distracts from your message.

By incorporating these advanced presentation techniques, you can elevate the impact and effectiveness of your presentations. Experiment with different approaches, evaluate audience feedback, and continuously refine your skills to create memorable and impactful presentations.

Customizing Slide Layouts and Designs

By taking the time to customize your slides, you can enhance the overall look and feel of your presentation, making it more professional, cohesive, and memorable. Here are some tips for customizing slide layouts and designs:

1. **Use Consistent Branding**: Incorporate your company or personal branding elements into your presentation design. Use your brand colors, logo, and fonts consistently throughout the slides to create a cohesive and professional look. This helps to reinforce your brand identity and makes your presentation visually aligned with your brand.

2. **Choose a Clean and Uncluttered Layout**: Avoid overcrowding your slides with too much text or visual elements. Opt for clean and uncluttered layouts that allow the content to stand out. Use white space effectively to create balance and improve readability. Remember that simplicity is key when it comes to slide designs.

3. **Select Suitable Fonts**: Choose fonts that are legible and appropriate for your presentation. Stick to one or two fonts to maintain a consistent look and feel. Avoid using decorative or overly stylized fonts that may be difficult to read on screen. Make sure your font sizes are large enough to be easily read from a distance.

4. **Utilize High-Quality Images:** Include high-quality and relevant images in your presentation to enhance visual appeal. Avoid using low-resolution or stretched images that may appear pixelated or distorted. Make sure your images are properly aligned and sized within the slide.

5. **Incorporate Visual Elements**: Use visual elements such as icons, charts, graphs, and infographics to present data or complex information in a more visually appealing and understandable way. These elements can help break up text-heavy slides and make your content more engaging.

6. **Apply Slide Transitions and Animations**: Add subtle slide transitions and animations to your presentation to create a dynamic and visually interesting experience. However, use them sparingly and purposefully to avoid overwhelming your audience or distracting from your message.

7. **Create Custom Slide Layouts**: Customize slide layouts to match the content and purpose of each slide. For example, you can create a unique layout for a title slide, bulleted lists, image-heavy slides, or quotes. This allows you to optimize the design for each type of content and make it more visually appealing and organized.

8. **Experiment with Color Schemes**: Choose a color scheme that matches your brand or theme. Use complementary colors to create a visually pleasing contrast. Be mindful of color psychology and choose colors that evoke the desired emotions or reactions from your audience. Stick to a limited color palette to maintain a cohesive and professional look.

9. **Use Grids and Alignment Tools**: Utilize grids and alignment tools within your presentation software to ensure your content is properly aligned and organized. This helps create a clean and polished look and makes your slides more visually appealing.

10. **Seek Inspiration and Templates**: Look for design inspiration from other presentations, websites, or design resources. You can also use pre-designed presentation templates that can provide a professional and cohesive design framework. Customize these templates to fit your specific content and brand.

Remember, customizing slide layouts and designs should be done purposefully and strategically, focusing on enhancing the visual appeal and readability of your content. By paying attention to these customization techniques, you can create visually stunning presentations that captivate and engage your audience.

Creating and Using Custom Templates

Creating and using custom templates can significantly streamline your presentation creation process and ensure consistency across your slides. Templates allow you to establish a predefined structure, layout, and design that can be easily applied to future presentations.
Here are some steps to creating and using custom templates effectively:

1. **Define Your Branding**: Before creating a custom template, clearly define your branding elements such as colors, fonts, and logos. These elements should align with your company or personal brand and be consistent across all your materials. This will serve as the foundation for your custom template.

2. **Design Your Master Slide**: Start by designing your master slide, which acts as the template for all your slides. This slide should include your branding elements, headers, footers, and any other repeating elements that will appear on every slide. It sets the overall look and feel of your presentation and ensures consistency throughout.

3. **Customize Other Slide Layouts**: After designing your master slide, customize the layouts for different types of slides, such as title slides, content slides, image slides, and so on. Each layout should have a consistent design while allowing flexibility for different content types. For example, a content slide layout may have a title section, subheadings, bullet points, and space for images or charts.

4. **Save as a Template**: Once your custom template is designed, save it as a template file (.potx in PowerPoint). This file will serve as the basis for future presentations. Make sure to give it a descriptive name and save it in a location where it can be easily accessed.

5. **Use Your Custom Template**: Whenever you start a new presentation, open your custom template. This will automatically apply the predefined structure, layout, and design to your slides. You can then focus on adding your content without worrying about the visual aspect. The template will ensure consistency and save time.

6. **Customize Slides as Necessary**: While using the template, you can still make modifications to individual slides as needed. For example, you may want to change the background image, adjust the font size, or add unique elements. However, try to maintain a consistent overall look and feel to uphold the branding and template.

7. **Update and Revise Templates**: Periodically review and update your custom templates to reflect any changes in branding or design trends. This will ensure that your templates stay relevant and effective. Pay attention to feedback from colleagues or clients to improve your templates and make adjustments as necessary.

8. **Share and Collaborate**: Custom templates are not limited to personal use. You can share them with colleagues or team members to maintain consistency across presentations within your organization. Consider establishing guidelines and best practices for using the templates to ensure everyone follows the same visual standards.

9. **Keep Evolving**: As you gain more experience and develop a better understanding of your presentation needs, you can continuously refine and evolve your custom templates. It's an iterative process, and you can always make improvements to optimize your templates for maximum impact.

By creating and using custom templates, you can save time, maintain consistency, and create visually appealing presentations that align with your brand. Templates provide a framework that allows you to focus on content creation rather than starting from scratch with each new presentation. Customize your templates to fit your needs and keep them up to date as your branding and design preferences evolve.

Advanced Animation and Slide Transition Effects

Using advanced animation and slide transition effects can enhance the visual impact and engagement of your presentations. Here are some tips on how to effectively utilize these features:

1. **Enhance Key Points**: Animation can be used to emphasize important points or information on a slide. For example, you can apply entrance effects to bullets or text boxes to make them appear one by one as you speak about them. This can help keep your audience focused and draw attention to specific content.

2. **Avoid Overuse**: While animations can be captivating, it's important not to overdo it. Excessive or unnecessary animations can be distracting or even annoying for your audience. Use animations sparingly and purposefully, only when they add value and help convey your message.

3. **Sync Animations with Delivery:** Time your animations to align with your speech or narration. This synchronization can help reinforce your message and create a more engaging presentation. Practice the timing of your animations in advance so you can smoothly transition between slides and content.

4. **Use Slide Transitions Wisely:** Slide transitions are the effects applied when moving from one slide to another. They can help create a seamless flow between slides and transitions. Choose subtle transition effects that are not too distracting but still add a touch of professionalism and sophistication to your presentation.

5. **Focus Audience Attention**: Animation can be used to guide your audience's attention to specific areas of the slide. For example, you can use motion path animations to draw arrows or lines that point to important elements on the slide. This can help direct the audience's focus and ensure they don't miss critical information.

6. **Maintain Consistency**: When using animation and slide transitions, try to maintain consistency throughout your presentation. Use the same effects or styles across slides to create a cohesive visual experience. This will make your presentation feel polished and professional.

7. **Test and Preview**: Before presenting, take the time to test your animations and slide transitions. Preview your presentation to ensure the timing and effects are working as intended. Make adjustments as needed to ensure a smooth and seamless presentation.

8. **Adapt to Audience Preferences**: Consider your audience's preferences and the context of your presentation when deciding whether to use advanced animations and slide transitions. Some audiences may prefer a more straightforward and minimalistic approach, while others may appreciate dynamic and visually exciting effects. Tailor your use of advanced features to suit your audience and the purpose of your presentation.

Remember, the goal of using advanced animation and slide transition effects is to enhance your content and engage your audience. Use them thoughtfully and strategically to support the delivery of your message and avoid overwhelming or distracting your audience.

Interactivity with Hyperlinks and Action Buttons

Adding interactivity to your presentations can greatly enhance engagement and make your content more dynamic. One way to achieve this is by utilizing hyperlinks and action buttons.
Here are some tips on how to effectively incorporate them into your presentations:

1. **Create Navigation**: Hyperlinks and action buttons can be used to create navigation within your presentation. Instead of linearly moving from one slide to another, you can create links or buttons that allow your audience to jump to specific sections or slides. This can help you structure your content in a non-linear way and allow your audience to explore the information at their own pace.

2. **Link External Sources**: Hyperlinks can be used to link to external sources such as websites, documents, or even other presentations. This can be useful when you want to provide additional resources or references for your audience to explore further. Make sure the links are relevant and add value to your presentation.

3. **Enable Interactive Elements:** Action buttons enable you to create interactive elements within your slides. For example, you can use an action button to reveal additional information, play videos, or trigger animations. This allows you to control the flow of information and engage your audience by allowing them to interact with the content.

4. **Create Interactive Quizzes or Surveys**: Hyperlinks and action buttons can be used to create interactive quizzes or surveys within your presentation. You can link to different slides with multiple-choice questions or use action buttons to reveal the correct answers. This can make your presentation more interactive and provide an opportunity for audience participation.

5. **Use Visual Cues**: When using hyperlinks or action buttons, it's important to provide visual cues to make them easily identifiable. Use consistent and intuitive design elements such as buttons, icons, or underlined text to indicate interactive elements. This will help your audience quickly identify and engage with those elements.

6. **Test and Preview**: Before presenting, thoroughly test your hyperlinks and action buttons to ensure they work as intended. Check that they navigate to the correct locations, trigger the correct actions, and function properly. Preview your presentation to make sure the interactivity flows smoothly and enhances the overall experience.

7. **Consider Accessibility**: When using hyperlinks and action buttons, consider the accessibility of your presentation. Ensure that the links and buttons are properly labeled and provide alternative text for visually impaired individuals who may be using screen readers. Make sure that your interactive elements are accessible to all audience members.

Remember, the key to adding interactivity with hyperlinks and action buttons is to enhance the engagement and learning experience for your audience. Use them strategically to provide additional information, enable interaction, or create a non-linear navigation structure. Be mindful of the purpose and context of your presentation to utilize these features effectively.

Collaborating and Sharing Presentations

Collaborating and sharing presentations with others can greatly enhance productivity, efficiency, and the quality of your work.

Here are some tips on how to effectively collaborate on and share presentations:

1. **Choose the Right Collaboration Tools**: There are several collaboration tools available that allow multiple users to work on a presentation simultaneously. Some popular options include Google Slides, Microsoft PowerPoint, and platforms like Dropbox or OneDrive. Choose a platform that suits your needs and offers real-time collaboration features.

2. **Define Roles and Responsibilities**: When collaborating on a presentation, it's important to define clear roles and responsibilities for each team member. Assign tasks, such as designing slides, researching content, or proofreading, based on each individual's skills and strengths. This will help streamline the workflow and ensure that everyone is working together towards a common goal.

3. **Establish Communication Channels**: Effective communication is crucial for successful collaboration. Set up regular meetings, either in person or through video conferencing tools, to discuss progress, address any issues, and provide feedback. Utilize communication tools such as email, chat apps, or project management platforms to stay connected and share updates in real-time.

4. **Use Version Control:** When multiple people are working on a presentation, it's important to have a system in place for version control. This ensures that changes made by different team members are tracked and can be easily identified. Use features like revision history or track changes to keep track of edits and collaborate seamlessly.

5. **Share Access and Permissions:** When sharing presentations, be mindful of the access and permissions you grant to collaborators. Different tools offer different sharing options, such as view-only, comment-only, or edit access. Determine the appropriate level of access for each collaborator based on their role and the level of involvement required.

6. **Encourage Feedback and Collaboration**: Collaboration is not just about completing individual tasks in isolation. Encourage open communication and seek feedback from your collaborators. This fosters a collaborative mindset and allows for the collective sharing of ideas and expertise, ultimately improving the quality of the presentation.

7. **Ensure Formatting Consistency**: When multiple people are working on different sections of a presentation, it's important to ensure formatting consistency. Establish guidelines for font styles, colors, spacing, and overall design to maintain a cohesive and professional look throughout the presentation. Regularly review and adjust formatting as needed to ensure consistency.

8. **Securely Share the Final Presentation**: Once the presentation is ready, securely share it with your intended audience. Depending on the sensitivity of the information, you may need to use password protection or encryption to safeguard the content. Choose a secure file-sharing method such as email attachments, cloud storage, or password-protected platforms.

Collaborating and sharing presentations can greatly enhance the outcome of your work. By utilizing the right tools, establishing clear communication channels, defining roles, and ensuring version control, you can successfully collaborate with others and produce high-quality presentations together.

Sharing Presentations via Email or Online Platforms

Sharing presentations via email or online platforms has become increasingly common in today's collaborative work environment. Here are some tips on how to effectively share presentations through these channels:

Email:

1. **Compress the Presentation**: To ensure smooth transmission, compress the presentation file into a smaller size before attaching it to an email. Many applications, such as Microsoft PowerPoint, offer options to compress the file while maintaining its quality.

2. **Use Cloud Storage Links**: Instead of attaching large presentation files directly to an email, consider uploading the file to a cloud storage platform like Google Drive, Dropbox, or OneDrive. Share a link to the presentation in the email, allowing recipients to access the file and collaborate on it.

3. **Add Clear Instructions:** When sharing a presentation via email, provide clear instructions to your recipients regarding the purpose of the presentation, the tasks you would like them to complete, and any specific deadlines or expectations.

4. **Consider Email Size Limits**: Be mindful of email size limits imposed by email providers, as large files may not be delivered or may cause delivery delays. If your presentation exceeds the limit, consider using a file-sharing service or splitting the file into multiple parts.

Online Platform:

1. **Collaborative Presentation Tools**: Platforms like Google Slides, Microsoft PowerPoint Online, Prezi, and SlideShare offer features specifically designed for online collaboration. Upload your presentation to one of these platforms and invite collaborators to access and edit the presentation simultaneously.

2. **Set Access and Editing Privileges**: When using an online platform, manage access and editing privileges for your presentation. Determine who can view, comment, or edit the presentation to ensure the right level of involvement for each collaborator.

3. **Version Control**: Online platforms often include version control features, allowing you to keep track of edits and revert to previous versions if needed. Take advantage of these features to maintain a clear history of changes and ensure a smooth collaborative process.

4. **Share Presentation Links**: Instead of emailing the presentation file, share a link to the online platform where the presentation is hosted. This way, collaborators can access and interact with the presentation directly from their web browser, eliminating the need for file downloads and potential version conflicts.

Whether through email attachments or online platforms, sharing presentations in a collaborative manner can greatly enhance the productivity and efficiency of your team. Choose the method that best suits your needs and ensure clear communication and access control throughout the collaboration process.

Collaborating with others in real-time using PowerPoint Online

Collaborating with others in real-time using PowerPoint Online allows for a seamless and efficient way to work together on presentations.

Here are some tips on how to effectively collaborate with others using PowerPoint Online:

1. **Share the Presentation**: Start by uploading your PowerPoint presentation to a cloud storage platform that supports real-time collaboration, such as OneDrive or SharePoint. Once uploaded, share the presentation with your collaborators by sending them a link or inviting them through their email addresses.

2. **Assign Roles and Permissions:** Determine the roles and permissions for each collaborator. PowerPoint Online allows you to set different levels of access and editing rights, such as view-only, comment, or edit. Assigning appropriate permissions ensures that each collaborator can contribute to the presentation according to their role.

3. **Collaborate in Real-time**: Once the presentation is shared, collaborators can access it simultaneously through their web browsers. Make sure all collaborators are aware of this so they understand that multiple people can be making edits and contributing at the same time.

4. **Communication**: Effective communication is key to successful collaboration. Use the chat feature provided in PowerPoint Online to interact with other collaborators in real-time. This helps to clarify any doubts, provide feedback, or discuss changes being made to the presentation.

5. **Review and Track Changes**: PowerPoint Online allows you to review and track the changes made by each collaborator. Utilize the "Review" tab to see a detailed history of modifications, accept or reject changes, and easily navigate through various versions of the presentation.

6. **Commenting and Feedback**: Collaborators can leave comments directly on specific slides or elements in PowerPoint Online. Encourage everyone to provide feedback, suggestions, or ask questions through comments. This maintains a clear record of discussions and ensures that important points are addressed.

7. **Save and Sync**: PowerPoint Online automatically saves changes in real-time. However, it's always a good practice to save the presentation manually at regular intervals. This ensures that all updates are synchronized across all collaborators' screens.

8. **Offline Access**: PowerPoint Online also allows collaborators to work on the presentation offline if they have the desktop version of PowerPoint installed. Any changes made will be synced back to the online version once the collaborator is back online.

Real-time collaboration using PowerPoint Online enhances productivity and allows for efficient teamwork. By following these tips, you can ensure a smooth and effective collaborative experience, whether you're working on a project with a small group or collaborating with a larger team.

Reviewing and Commenting on Presentations

Reviewing and commenting on presentations is an essential part of the collaborative process.
Here are some tips on how to effectively review and provide feedback on presentations:

1. **Read the Presentation**: Take the time to thoroughly read and understand the presentation before providing feedback. Familiarize yourself with the content, structure, and overall message of the presentation.

2. **Focus on Objectives**: Keep the objectives and goals of the presentation in mind while reviewing. Make sure that the content aligns with the intended purpose and that the message is clear and compelling.

3. **Provide Constructive Feedback**: When leaving comments or providing feedback, be specific and constructive. Point out areas of improvement, suggest alternative approaches, and highlight strengths. Remember to maintain a positive and supportive tone.

4. **Comment on Structure and Flow**: Evaluate the organization and flow of the presentation. Check if the information is logically arranged, transitions between slides are smooth, and if the overall structure supports the central message.

5. **Check for Clarity and Conciseness**: Pay attention to the clarity and conciseness of the presentation. Ensure that the information is easily understandable, avoid jargon or technical language if it can be confusing, and consider if any points need further clarification.

6. **Review Visuals and Design Elements**: Evaluate the visuals, such as graphs, charts, images, and font choices. Check if they enhance the content and support the message effectively. Provide feedback on the layout, color scheme, and overall design of the slides.

7. **Consistency and Formatting**: Ensure that there is consistency in formatting throughout the presentation. Check for consistent font sizes, styles, and formatting of bullets, headers, and footers. Inconsistent formatting can be distracting and may negatively impact the overall impression.

8. **Proofread for Errors**: Pay attention to grammatical, spelling, and punctuation errors. Spelling mistakes and grammatical errors can detract from the professionalism of the presentation. Be sure to highlight any errors you notice, especially if they may impact the accuracy or clarity of the content.

9. **Prioritize Important Feedback**: If you have multiple comments or suggestions, prioritize the most critical or impactful ones. It's important to provide focused feedback rather than overwhelming the presenter with too many changes or suggestions.

10. **Review and Discuss Changes**: Once your feedback has been shared, collaborate with others involved in the presentation to discuss the recommended changes. Address any questions or concerns, and work together to refine the presentation further.

Remember, the goal of reviewing and commenting on presentations is to help improve the overall quality and effectiveness of the content. By following these tips, you can provide valuable feedback and contribute to the success of the presentation.

Protecting Presentations with Passwords and Permissions

Protecting presentations with passwords and permissions is essential to ensure the security and confidentiality of sensitive information.
Here are some tips on how to effectively protect your presentations:

1. **Use Strong Passwords**: When setting a password for your presentation, use a strong and unique combination of alphanumeric characters, symbols, and upper and lowercase letters. Avoid common or easily guessable passwords.

2. **Limit Access**: Only share your presentation with individuals who need to see it. By limiting access to a select few, you reduce the chances of unauthorized parties viewing or modifying your presentation.

3. **Encrypt the Presentation**: Many presentation software tools provide the option to encrypt presentations. Encryption converts the data into a format that can only be unlocked with a specific password or encryption key, protecting the content from unauthorized access.

4. **Set Permissions**: Take advantage of the permissions settings provided by presentation software. These features allow you to control what actions can be performed on the presentation, such as editing, copying, or printing. Set appropriate permissions based on the needs of each user.

5. **Consider Watermarking**: Watermarking can deter unauthorized distribution or plagiarism of your presentation. Add a watermark with your name, organization, or a copyright symbol to each slide, making it clear that the presentation is confidential and should not be shared without permission.

6. **Regularly Update Passwords**: To maintain security, update passwords periodically. It is best practice to change passwords every few months or as

needed, especially if you suspect unauthorized access or if there is a change in personnel who have access to the presentation.

7. **Be Wary of Public Networks**: Avoid accessing or sharing your password-protected presentations on public or unsecured networks. Public Wi-Fi networks can be vulnerable to hacking and eavesdropping, increasing the risk of unauthorized access to your sensitive information.

8. **Secure Storage**: Store your presentations in a secure location, whether it be on an encrypted hard drive, a cloud storage service with strong security measures, or on a protected internal server. Regularly backup your presentations to prevent data loss.

9. **Educate Users**: If multiple individuals have access to the presentation, educate them about the importance of maintaining security and the need to protect the presentation's password and permissions. Emphasize the importance of not sharing passwords or granting unauthorized access.

10. **Regularly Audit Access**: Periodically review who has access to your presentation and evaluate if they still require access. Remove access for individuals who no longer need it, reducing the risk of unauthorized users accessing or modifying the presentation.

By implementing these measures, you can enhance the security and confidentiality of your presentations, protecting sensitive information and ensuring that only authorized individuals can access and modify the content.

Steps involves in Protecting Presentations with Passwords and Permissions

Here are step-by-step instructions on protecting presentations with passwords and permissions:

1. Open the presentation in your presentation software (e.g., Microsoft PowerPoint, Google Slides).

2. Locate the option for password protection or encryption. This option is usually found under the "File" or "Tools" menu. In Microsoft PowerPoint, for example, it is under "File" > "Protect Presentation" > "Encrypt with Password".

3. Select the password protection or encryption option. This will prompt you to enter a password.

4. Enter a strong and unique password. Make sure it meets the recommended password requirements (e.g., a combination of alphanumeric characters, symbols, and a mix of upper and lowercase letters).

5. Confirm the password by entering it again.

6. Save the presentation. The presentation is now password protected and cannot be opened without entering the designated password.

7. Set permissions for the presentation. This step may vary depending on the presentation software you are using. In Microsoft PowerPoint, for instance, you can go to "File" > "Protect Presentation" > "Restrict Permission" > "Restricted Access".

8. Specify the permissions you want to grant to different users or groups. You can choose options such as read-only access, editing access, copying, or

printing permissions. Specify the appropriate permissions for each individual or group.

9. Set a unique password or authorization for each user or group who will have access to the presentation. This is usually done by clicking on the "Add..." button or a similar option and entering the user's name or email address.

10. Save the permissions settings. The presentation is now password protected and access is restricted to certain individuals or groups based on the permissions you have set.

11. Test the password protection and permissions by trying to access the presentation with the designated password or by attempting different actions based on the assigned permissions.

Remember to regularly update the passwords and permissions as needed and to educate users on the importance of maintaining the security of the presentation.

Course Conclusion

Upon completion of this training course, participants will have a comprehensive understanding of Microsoft PowerPoint and its capabilities. They will be able to create professional and visually appealing presentations, effectively communicate ideas and information, and enhance the impact and engagement of their slides. The skills acquired in this course will be valuable in various professional settings, including business, education, and training.

GENERAL CONCLUSION ON MICROSOFT OFFICE PACKAGES

The use of Microsoft Office packages such as Word, Excel, and PowerPoint provides users with essential tools for efficient document creation, data analysis, and impactful presentations.

By mastering these applications, individuals are empowered to enhance their productivity, communicate ideas effectively, and organize information in a professional and visually appealing manner.

The versatility and wide range of features offered by Microsoft Office make it a vital skill set for individuals across various industries and professions.

If you have indeed gone through these courses, congratulations. You now have to subscribe to Continuous learning and exploration of these packages for it will further enable you to leverage the full potential of these powerful tools already in your hands, ultimately leading to improved work efficiency and effectiveness in any workplace or environment you find yourself....